THE GOSPEL OF LUKE

THE GOSPEL OF MARY

THE GOSPEL OF MARY
A Month with the Mother of God

GABRIEL AMORTH, SSP

ALBA·HOUSE · NEW·YORK

SOCIETY OF ST. PAUL, 2187 VICTORY BLVD., STATEN ISLAND, NEW YORK 10314

ST PAULS

Originally published in Italian by Edizioni San Paolo, s.r.l. under the title
Il Vangelo di Maria.

Library of Congress Cataloging-in-Publication Data

    Amorth, Gabriele.
      [Vangelo di Maria. English]
      The Gospel of Mary: a month with the Mother of God / Gabriel
    Amorth; translated by Edmund C. Lane.
         p.   cm.
      ISBN 0-8189-0871-8
      1. Mary, Blessed Virgin, Saint — Biography Meditations. 2.
    Devotional calendars — Catholic Church. I. Title.
    BT605.2.A56   2000
    232.91 — dc21   99-30144
                                             CIP

Produced and designed in the United States of America by the
Fathers and Brothers of the Society of St. Paul,
2187 Victory Boulevard, Staten Island, New York 10314-6603,
as part of their communications apostolate.

ISBN: 0-8189-0871-8

Printing Information:

Current Printing - first digit   1   2   3   4   5   6   7   8   9   10

Year of Current Printing - first year shown

2000   2001   2002   2003   2004   2005   2006   2007   2008

Table of Contents

Introduction

When I was invited to write a "brief and simple" work for a Marian month, I thought that perhaps this book on the Madonna could make some small contribution for those who would be living in a new millennium. The Holy Father in his apostolic letter *Tertio millennio adveniente*, in which he outlined his program for the years leading up to the year 2000, entrusted to the Holy Spirit the job of preparing souls "to celebrate with renewed faith and generous participation in the great event...." And he went on to say: "I entrust this work of all the Church to the heavenly intercession of Mary, Mother of the Redeemer. She who is the Mother of all love, will be for Christians... the Star who guides their steps securely to their meeting with the Lord. May the humble daughter of Nazareth, who two thousand years ago offered to the world the Word Incarnate, direct the men and women of the new millennium to Him who is 'the true light, who enlightens every man' (Jn 1:9)."

It is good to think of Mary as a star who guides our steps securely to the Lord. The Magi followed the star and found Jesus with his mother. Let us ask the Virgin to take us by the hand and guide us.

In these pages, I have sought to retrace the journey which, following the pages of Sacred Scripture and the teaching of the Church, brings us to know the Mother of Jesus and our mother too. To know the Mother is to know the Son, because God has determined that the rapport between Mary and Jesus might exceed any natural relationship and that the Virgin might be the first of the redeemed, the first disciple, the first collaborator with his Divine Son.

I ask the Lord to bless this modest undertaking that, if it pleases Him, it might be able to do a modicum of good for the men and women of this new millennium.

Father Gabriel Amorth, SSP

Biblical Abbreviations

OLD TESTAMENT

Genesis	Gn	Nehemiah	Ne	Baruch	Ba
Exodus	Ex	Tobit	Tb	Ezekiel	Ezk
Leviticus	Lv	Judith	Jdt	Daniel	Dn
Numbers	Nb	Esther	Est	Hosea	Ho
Deuteronomy	Dt	1 Maccabees	1 M	Joel	Jl
Joshua	Jos	2 Maccabees	2 M	Amos	Am
Judges	Jg	Job	Jb	Obadiah	Ob
Ruth	Rt	Psalms	Ps	Jonah	Jon
1 Samuel	1 S	Proverbs	Pr	Micah	Mi
2 Samuel	2 S	Ecclesiastes	Ec	Nahum	Na
1 Kings	1 K	Song of Songs	Sg	Habakkuk	Hab
2 Kings	2 K	Wisdom	Ws	Zephaniah	Zp
1 Chronicles	1 Ch	Sirach	Si	Haggai	Hg
2 Chronicles	2 Ch	Isaiah	Is	Malachi	Ml
Ezra	Ezr	Jeremiah	Jr	Zechariah	Zc
		Lamentations	Lm		

NEW TESTAMENT

Matthew	Mt	Ephesians	Eph	Hebrews	Heb
Mark	Mk	Philippians	Ph	James	Jm
Luke	Lk	Colossians	Col	1 Peter	1 P
John	Jn	1 Thessalonians	1 Th	2 Peter	2 P
Acts	Ac	2 Thessalonians	2 Th	1 John	1 Jn
Romans	Rm	1 Timothy	1 Tm	2 John	2 Jn
1 Corinthians	1 Cor	2 Timothy	2 Tm	3 John	3 Jn
2 Corinthians	2 Cor	Titus	Tt	Jude	Jude
Galatians	Gal	Philemon	Phm	Revelation	Rv

THE GOSPEL OF MARY

The New Woman

When every year on the 8th of September the Church celebrates the liturgical feast of the Birth of Mary, the overriding thought is that the dawn has broken announcing the day of the Lord: the birth of the Virgin Mary is the prelude to the birth of Jesus. The Second Vatican Council spoke of the birth of the Virgin in a very felicitous way. Chapter eight of the Constitution on the Church *Lumen gentium* (LG), wholly dedicated to the Virgin Mary, affirms in paragraph 55: "With her, the incomparable Daughter of Zion, after having long awaited the promise, the time was fulfilled and a new economy was begun."

To understand the role of Mary and how her appearance signaled a decisive turn in the unfolding of the plan of salvation, it is necessary to begin with some concept regarding the divine plan of creation and hence of the absolute centrality of Christ. He is the first born of all creation; everything was made for him and in view of him. He is the center of creation, the one who would recapitulate in himself all creatures: those celestial (the angels) and those terrestrial (humankind). I think that no matter what, Jesus would have become flesh and would have appeared triumphant on earth; but it is difficult to prove. The reality is another thing. After the sin of our first parents, which enslaved humankind to Satan and to the consequences of their sin (suffering, fatigue, sickness, and death), Jesus came as a savior to redeem humankind, through his blood and the cross, from the consequences of sin and to reconcile to God all things in heaven and on the earth.

All was created in view of Christ. On this Christocentric point the role of every creature, of each one of us already present in the thought of God from all eternity, depends. If the first born of every creature is the Word Incarnate, it is impossible not to associate with him, before any other creature in the thought of God, the woman through whom such an incarnation would be brought about. In this is to be found the unique relationship between Mary and the Most Holy Trinity, as is clearly manifested in the page of the Annunciation.

The centrality of Christ and his coming as savior is key to everything. The whole of human history is thus oriented to the birth of Jesus, which is referred to as "the fullness of time." The centuries preceding his coming are "times of expectation"; the centuries following are "the end times." With the birth of Mary human history takes a great turn. The period of waiting is ended and the period of realization begins. She is the new Woman, the new Eve; from her is to come the Redeemer and a new people of God is inaugurated. The very first of the Fathers of the Church, like Justin and Irenaeus like to compare Eve and Mary. Eve was the mother of the living; Mary, the Mother of the redeemed. Eve gave to humankind the fruit of death; Mary gave to humanity Christ, the fruit of life.

At this point we would like to point out several details regarding Mary, but we find ourselves without much of the information that we need. The Gospels are not historical-biographical books; they are historical-salvific books. They are the preaching of the "good news." We do not find in them those things that would be solely of human interest, with no value with regard to salvation. Because of this we find a lack of much news which would be of interest to us because of their biographical value, but which have no importance with regard to the goal of the message which the evangelists wanted to pass on to us.

Let us take a look at some of these questions, without any claim to finding any certain response, but which we can come close to an

2

answer to through approximation, or at least we can become more aware of the reasons behind certain choices made by the evangelists.

When was the Madonna born? As far as the day is concerned, in ancient times several different dates were given, always suggested by cultic rather than by historical motives. Eventually the date of September 8th prevailed, even if it was unfounded historically, and from this, the date of her conception nine months earlier, the feast of the Immaculate Conception was determined. As far as the year is concerned, we can only guess from the date of the birth of Jesus, also uncertain, but which can be approximated pretty closely. By taking into account the fact that young girls were married between the ages of 12 and 14, it is tempting to think that the Madonna may have been born in the year 20 B.C., when Herod the Great began the reconstruction of the Temple in Jerusalem. It is tempting because, while man was building a temple of stone, God was preparing his true temple of flesh. But this is just probable, even if it is a date close to the real one which we do not know for sure.

Where was the Madonna born? Among the various hypotheses that have been put forth regarding the possible cities which may have been the birthplace of Mary, the two most probable which are in contention for this honor are Jerusalem and Nazareth. Both boast of a very ancient tradition, with archeological and cultic proofs. We lean toward Nazareth, since it was there that we first meet the humble handmaid of the Lord, surrounded by the greatest possible obscurity: a hilly place which had 200 inhabitants (more or less) who lived in caves, at whose entrance a small room may have been added. Outside the lines of communication, Nazareth is not even named in the Old Testament, nor in the Talmud, nor by Flavius Josephus. "What good ever came out of Nazareth?" Nathaniel would say to Philip.

About Mary we don't even know to which of the twelve tribes of Israel her family may have belonged. It surely must have been a very humble tribe; otherwise St. Luke would certainly have said so since he took pains to refer to the family of Elizabeth and of Anna, the other two women of whom he speaks in the Gospel of Christ's infancy. God prizes humility and obscurity. He doesn't know what to make of human greatness which only counts in the eyes of men.

Reflections

About Mary — "Humble and great, more than a creature," was the way Dante defined her. She possessed none of the requisites of human greatness. Her sole value lies in the fact that she was chosen by God to play a role of superior importance to any human exaltation whatsoever (who has the power to raise a woman to the dignity of Mother of God?) and she always corresponded fully, with intelligence and freedom, to the will of her Lord.

About us — Each one of us has also been thought of by God from all eternity and must accomplish that salvific role, for ourselves and for others, which God assigns to us and makes known to us through the various circumstances of our lives, as well as through the "talents" (material goods and personal gifts) which we have received from the Lord. Our greatness will depend on how we correspond and how we stand before the eyes of God.

You Are All Holy, Mary

From all eternity God has thought of each one of us. He has assigned to each of us a specific role and caused us to be born at just the right time and in just the right place, providing us with those gifts which would be necessary for us to fulfill our role. Thus he did with Mary. Wanting to entrust her with a truly extraordinary work, he prepared her for its obligations. We can sum up that preparation in three words which will be the object of our reflections in this chapter and in the two which follow: Immaculate, Virgin, Spouse of Joseph.

The first present, the great gift which God gave to Mary at the very moment of her conception was that of making her immaculate, applying to her in anticipation the merits of the redemption of Christ. She was to become the mother of him who would come to destroy the works of Satan, namely sin and all its consequences. So Mary, conceived immaculate, manifests her equality with us, because she too had need of being redeemed by the sacrifice of the cross; on the other hand, her immaculate state predisposed her for the exalted mission which would then be offered to her.

One of the most ancient of the Marian titles to this day is held in particular esteem among the Orthodox and that is "All Holy." It expresses well the two aspects that it hopes to convey when Mary is called Immaculate. The first aspect is that of pure privilege, the exemption from Original Sin in view of her divine maternity. Here we can only contemplate the marvels worked by the Lord. But there is more, there is a second aspect in which it is affirmed that Mary never committed the smallest actual sin, even though she was an intelligent and free creature. Contrary to all appearances, we touch in this Mary's inimitability which can have such a powerful influence on our Christian formation: we see in Mary the beauty of human nature suffused by grace. The Immaculata is an ideal which draws us without dazzling us; it does not distance the figure of Mary from us, but encourages us to imitate her with our baptismal and actual graces in our fight against sin.

One of the greatest sins against humanity of our modern mentality is that of wanting to remove the sense of sin and of the awesome presence of Satan. In this way we misunderstand the redemption which is the victory of Christ over sin and the devil. In this way we leave fallen humankind in its misery and do nothing to help lift it out, to become better, to reacquire its original beauty as creatures formed in the image and likeness of God. The Immaculata says to us: I am the way I am by the grace of Christ and my correspondence to it; you too must try, by corresponding to grace, to conquer evil and to purify yourself ever more. The Immaculata is not an abstract ideal to contemplate; she is a model to imitate.

It is good, too, to review the long road which led finally to the dogmatic definition of the Immaculate Conception in 1854. The sensibilities of believers from the very beginning intuited the total sanctity of Mary and exalted her in conformity with her own prophecy: "Henceforth all generations will call me blessed" (Lk 1:48). It is to be noted that in proclaiming Mary "All Holy," we wanted above all to underscore that she never committed any actual sin; and it was in this sense that the Council of Trent used the phrase. But even before this, the reflection and conviction of the People of God had gone even further and had intuited that the total sanctity of Mary was incompatible with Original Sin, from which she must certainly have been excluded.

With regard to this truth, the biblical and theological reflection needed greater depth. We know that dogmas are "firm points of reference" which do not block further studies and enrichment, but rather point them in the right direction. We know that the dogmatic proclamation of a truth means that it is somehow contained in Sacred Scripture. But not all truths are contained with the same clarity; some are explicitly affirmed (one thinks for example of the resurrection of Christ), others are contained only implicitly and time is required along with the light of the Holy Spirit to reveal them. For this reason hesitation and difficulty should not surprise us. We should note that St. Thomas Aquinas, when it came to the matter of the Immaculate Conception, was against the proposition because he feared that in some way it would mean that the Virgin Mary was excluded from redemption; it would be for her a wrong, not an exaltation. His doubt was real and well founded, and it was necessary to resolve it. And Duns Scotus did resolve it by understanding that Mary had to have been redeemed by the merits of Christ which were preventively applied to her. Thus Mary is the first and the most beautiful fruit of the redemption.

Another question which is often posed is: Was the Madonna ever tempted by Satan and could she have sinned? Certainly the Virgin, like all of us, had the gift of freedom which the Lord gave and respects in all his superior creatures. In the past, when it was popular to exalt the privileges of Mary, it was thought that Mary had a "moral impossibility" of ever sinning. As far as the temptations of the Devil are concerned, as we saw with Jesus, certainly Mary was likewise tempted even if the Gospel does not speak of it, since this is a condition of our human nature even before the Original Sin. Today, insisting less on extraordinary gifts, it is more popular to focus the spotlight on the more human aspects of Mary: her difficult walk of faith, her continual sufferings. The encyclical letter of Pope John Paul II, *Redemptoris Mater*, follows along these lines. But it also throws light on two other considerations:

1. To be able to sin is not necessary for freedom; the angels and the saints are fully free, even if they are sinless.

2. The fruits of the redemption were fully, if preventively, applied to the Madonna. Even with us the redemption will have reached its full complement when, having achieved celestial glory, while remaining intelligent and free creatures, we will no longer have the possibility of committing sin.

Reflections

About Mary — She corresponded perfectly to the graces which were accorded her in full. Conceived immaculate in light of her divine maternity, she then became the most faithful listener and disciple of her Son. The sanctity of Mary, which approaches that of Jesus as closely as is possible to any human creature, never in fact exempted her from the difficult walk of faith, from suffering, or from the most bloody crosses.

About us — The Immaculate Conception invites us to a constant battle against sin. It invites us to better ourselves and to make of our lives a continuous journey towards conversion and purification, of tending toward that holiness of life to which God calls each of us. Jesus invites us to be holy as our heavenly Father is holy, perfect as the Father is perfect and merciful as the Father is merciful. The Immaculata tells us that it is possible, with God's grace, to succeed in approximating the holiness of God as much as is allowed to a human creature.

Thrice a Virgin

There is an apocryphal book, highly authoritative on account of its antiquity which may go back as far as the first decade of the 2nd century, the *Protogospel of James*. From this book we learn the names of Mary's parents, Joachim and Anna. We also learn of other episodes which however must be understood in the proper sense. The key to the reading of this book is to recognize the fact that it was written to teach us some truth through the use of invented stories. It's a little like an instructor who teaches children through the use of fables which contain some real truth. When this ancient author tells us that Mary at the age of three was presented in the Temple to be instructed there, he wants to let us know that in reality Mary, from the time she had the use of reason, offered herself as a temple of God. Thus the celebration on the 21st of November, which bears the solemn title of "The Presentation of the Blessed Virgin Mary," and which was initiated in 543 with the dedication of the basilica of St. Mary in Jerusalem, is in reality the feast of the virginity of Mary.

Even virginity is a gift of God when it is chosen in order for one to belong to him alone and to keep oneself entirely for his disposal. It is a gift which the Spirit gave to Mary, as he had given her the gift of her immaculate conception. We affirm this because the history of Israel does not present us with anything of this sort. It was never even thought of that consecrated virginity might be a state of life pleasing to God, and all the great women of Israel, held up as examples and thus, under certain aspects, forerunners of the Madonna (Sarah, Deborah, Judith, Esther, etc.), were either married or widowed. Israel only prized motherhood; the lack of children was considered a matter of shame, a curse, a rebuke on the part of God.

How could the Virgin, with a courage that has no human explanation, have ever conceived the idea of remaining a virgin? Later, of course, Jesus would teach what was more perfect and a whole company of men and women down through the ages would live lives of virginity entirely consecrated to God. But the Madonna did not have before her eyes a single model of this type. Only the Holy Spirit could have suggested to her a choice so out of the ordinary and to have given her the strength to follow it. Perhaps she had begun to understand, from the time she had the use of reason, the grand precept continually repeated by pious Israelites: "You shall love the Lord your God with all your heart, with all your soul and with all your strength" and wanted to live it in an absolute way. But it is useless to want to seek a human explanation for a divine choice. I believe that even here Mary must have had a premonition of the teachings of Jesus and was truly "the daughter of her Son," as Dante calls her.

I also believe that she must have acted with complete spontaneity and simplicity: without taking into account that she was following a new way and opening up a new avenue; without worrying about how she would live this choice so totally without precedent, above all when her parents had given her in marriage to Joseph. It is Mary's style to have absolute faith, without creating problems for herself or asking for an explanation, but abandoning herself entirely into the hands of the Lord. Pope Paul VI underscores another aspect: through her choice of virginity, Mary did not renounce any human value whatsoever. To follow the way of virginity never takes away from the value of matrimony nor does it ever set a limit to that holiness to which we are all called. It is rather to follow with generosity a particular vocation of the Lord.

Mary was thrice a virgin: before, during and after giving birth. It is necessary to exalt her virginity in this world which at times seems so confused, with the consequences that not only are we suffering from a frightful lack of vocations, but the unity of the family is also too often destroyed. We seem to live in a world so mundane, so immersed in sex and violence, that vice moves about our streets with head held high, often defended by permissive laws, while it seems that virtue must hide itself in shame. But the judgment of God and the good of society are wholly on the other side.

There is no doubt that the virginity of Mary reminds us also of that virtue of purity which the Decalog defends in two command-ments which St. Paul almost identifies with holiness, illustrating in them the motives of faith as no one had ever done before. He goes beyond the idea of a simple domination of self, important but merely human, already held in high esteem by the pagans. It is important that women be respected for themselves, but it is just as important that they be the first to respect themselves! St. Paul invites us to a qualitative leap. Meanwhile let us note how impurity in the Bible is often indicated by the Greek word *porneia* (the first part, *porno*, is easily understood), which in turn is derived from a verb which means *to sell oneself*. St. Paul is moved to take this as his point of departure in suggesting three motives for faith, which include a horror of *porneia*, of impurity.

(1) You cannot sell yourself because you do not belong to yourself; you have been purchased by Jesus at a very high price, and hence you belong to him. We think of how clear the concept of ransoming a slave was in those times.

(2) You belong to Christ not as an external object or a piece of his property, but as a member of his body. Would you dare to take a piece of Christ, one of his members, and degrade it through prostitution, *porneia*?

(3) The body is sacred because it is a temple of the Holy Spirit. We think of how highly respected, among all religions, are its places of worship. Would you ever dare to profane the temple of the Holy Spirit? How could you commit this sacrilege? We have to recognize that no religion, no philosophy ever had such a high respect for the human body as Christianity: member of Christ, temple of the Holy Spirit, destined to a glorious resurrection.

"I believe in Jesus Christ, but I don't believe in the chastity of priests," a professional person once said to me. "My ideal is to become a porno star," a sixteen-year-old confided. "Father, pray for my son who is living with a married woman twenty years older than he," a mother pleaded. "How can it be: our daughter, a homebody and church-goer, now lives with a drug addicted boy and doesn't want to hear about coming back home," two parents said, venting their feelings. And I could go on and on. These are the facts of our day, while the newspapers seem to speak only of violence against women and children.

May our heavenly Mother, thrice virgin, she who is *the* Virgin par excellence, help us to heal our society with her immaculate purity. In all the Orthodox icons the thrice Virgin Mary is depicted with three stars, one on her forehead and the other two on her shoulders.

Reflections

About Mary — The candor of Mary is enchanting. The secret lies in her obedience to the call of the Holy Spirit: with humility and courage she challenged the ways of the world, fear of being misunderstood and despised, along with other difficulties which may have seemed to her insurmountable. But this is what Jesus wanted of his mother. Those who are preoccupied with pleasing God put their faith in his help and receive the grace they need to overcome obstacles which seem insuperable.

About us — The example of Mary is our model and her presence, intercession. Each one of us has to observe the virtue of chastity according to his or her state in life. The reminder of Paul: "Do not conform yourselves to the mentality of this world" (Rm 12:2) and the three motives of faith which we have just mentioned should urge us on to be the very best children of the Virgin we can be. "Blessed are the pure of heart [those who possess an interior, total and not only formal purity] because they shall see God" (Mt 5:8).

A Marriage Willed by God

We find ourselves reflecting now on the third prerequisite willed by God to prepare Mary for the incarnation of the Word: it was essential that the Mother forechosen, besides being immaculate and ever a virgin, be married. The motives are many and some of them are more than evident: a shelter, assistance, and education were necessary. It was also important that the Son of God, by experiencing an ordinary, often hidden life, should live in a real family, exemplary even if different, in conformity with the scope willed by God. And there was also the need to fulfill the messianic prophecies, for which the promised Messiah was to be a "son of David."

In those days young girls got married at a very early age, between 12 and 14; and the boys between 17 and 18. When we read that the daughter of Jairus, brought back to life by Jesus, was 12 years old, to us this detail only says that she was a youngster. Instead, a very important thing is being said here: she was in the flower of her youth when her father would be preoccupied in finding a husband for his daughter. Taking into account the customs of the time and the young age of the girl, it was up to the parents to arrange everything. At the proper time, the parents of the boy started looking for a young girl who would be suitable for their son, and the parents of the young girl would be seeking the right person to whom they could give her in marriage. The negotiations would begin and the

13

mohar, the dowry which the aspiring groom would have to pay to the parents of the bride, would be determined. It should be noted that, unlike with other people, the dowry was not considered a price for the bride; it was a small patrimony, a kind of guarantee, kept by the parents but belonging to the bride, which she would claim in case she were to become a widow or divorced.

At this point the marriage would take place in two stages. First, in the house of the bride and in the presence of close relatives, the declaration of the marriage with all its juridical effects would take place (it is improper to refer to this as an engagement). The blessing of the parents conferred a sacred character on this simple ceremony. A year later, during which time the spouses continued to live apart with their respective parents and during which the groom prepared a house for his new family, the solemn wedding ceremony would take place in which the bride was brought into the house of the groom, with all their relatives and friends present amid festivities which commonly would last seven days.

In keeping with these customs the marriage of Mary and Joseph would have taken place in this fashion. I doubt that Mary would have revealed to her parents her proposal to remain a virgin; the Jews, in the case of private vows, would have had to ask permission of parents or spouse. But it is Mary's style to keep quiet and to entrust herself entirely to the Lord, with a faith at some times heroic, as we see in this occasion and as we shall see in the Annunciation and at the foot of the cross, in spite of the evidence of the facts.

Now to Joseph, the spouse chosen by the Lord for her who was to become the Mother of God, through the parents. Right away the name recalls that of Joseph the Hebrew who saved from famine that first nucleus of the Hebrew people, formed from the large family of Jacob. Of St. Joseph, the Gospels will say three very important things.

First of all it tells us with insistence, both through Luke and then through Matthew, that he belongs to the family of David. It is a very important piece of information. The most significant episode in the life of King David is precisely when the Lord promised him that his house would last forever. The prophecy was at once understood in a messianic sense, even because the political importance of the family of David at the time of Jesus, had ceased some 500 years earlier with Zerubbabel. Luke and Matthew, in giving us the genealogy of Jesus, give us the genealogy of Joseph. It is clear that the marriage between Mary and Joseph is the link which puts into effect the prophecy in which the Messiah was to be a descendant of David. The true way to refer to Joseph is not "thought-to-be the father of Jesus" or "foster father of Jesus" or other such expressions; it is much better to call him the "Davidic father" of Jesus.

The Gospel provides us with a second piece of information regarding Joseph — his job: he was a carpenter or craftsman. We know, therefore, his economic situation and the condition in which the Holy Family would have lived, and that of Jesus himself with Mary after the death of Joseph. A craftsman was considered to be somewhere in the middle of his social class; poor, but not destitute. He lived by his daily work which would be complemented by what he was able to grow in his garden, the fruits of a small orchard, and some domestic animals.

A third piece of information is provided by Matthew who calls Joseph a "just" man. It is a term rich in biblical significance. It indicates great rectitude, full observance of the laws of God, openness and full availability to the divine will. There is no doubt that the parents of the two spouses would have chosen for their children the right person; and there is no doubt that the Holy Spirit would have assisted them in their decision.

The social status of Joseph, an honest and good artisan, gives us an idea also of the economic condition of Mary's family. In contrast to the fantastic tales of the apocryphal writings which made Mary an only daughter and rich heiress, it is clear that her family, too, was of modest means. It is also true that the life of the Holy Family would have been characterized by a dignified poverty, but not destitute. Humble the land in which they lived, humble the job of Joseph and then of Jesus; poor the condition in which they found themselves in Bethlehem, poor the offering which they made in the Temple on the occasion of the presentation of Jesus forty days after his birth. Mary and Joseph belonged to the "poor of Yahweh" which the Bible exalts because they abandoned themselves in faith to the Lord. The

Lord reveals himself to them and finds them open to realizing his great plans. The poverty which the Gospel calls "blessed," and which it holds up as a voluntary choice, is not an exaltation of pauperism and misery. It is a recognition of how much spiritual values are superior in comparison to the fleeting values which human nature tends to exalt. It encompasses faith in the divine promises and constant openness to accomplish the will of God, sought in his word and in the circumstances of one's life.

Reflections

About Mary — She doesn't remove herself from the customs of her people or from obedience to her parents. She knew how to see in all things the hand of God, contrary to all appearances. The evidence of the facts, that is her marriage to Joseph, seemed to interrupt and to annul her proposal of belonging fully to the Lord. She never ceased to trust that the Lord, if he wanted this of her, would have made it possible for her to observe virginity even in her marriage.

About us — Certainly the parents of Joseph chose well, and Joseph would have felt very happy in a place so small, where everyone knew everyone else very well. They did not look for wealth or ephemeral values, but virtue. There is no true love if not in the light of God and with the desire to fulfill his will, the mission that he has entrusted to us. Availability to accomplish the will of God never makes us feel frustrated, even if events take us away from our own plans and aspirations. Dante would say: "It is in your will, O God, that we find our peace."

Exult! Be Glad! Rejoice!

Immaculate, ever virgin, spouse of Joseph: Mary is now ready for the great annunciation of her mission. The event clearly takes place during the year of waiting prior to her wedding day, though the declaration of matrimony had already taken place making the young girl already the wife of Joseph for all intents and purposes even if normally, during this period, the couple would refrain from marital relations even though such would have been legitimate. The divine messenger powerfully breaks in on the life of the Virgin in a troubling way; the event took place almost certainly in her home, for which the inscription which we read both at Nazareth and at Loreto, maintaining that this was the place where the annunciation took place, is legitimate: "*Here* the Word was made flesh!"

Cháire, kecharitoméne: Exult, O highly favored of God. Be glad, you who have been filled to overflowing with divine grace. Rejoice, elect of God who has favored you above all others. Thus can we translate the salutation of the angel. They are words of great significance and explicit messianic import. For that reason they have the power to disturb the young girl; she understands that in these words is expressed an extraordinary plan on the part of God, but she does not fully comprehend what it all means. *Cháire* is not the usual Hebrew salutation, *shalom*, peace be with you; nor is it a simple *ave* (hail), or *salve* (be of good health), both of which have prevailed unfortunately in our translations. *Cháire* (exult, be glad, rejoice) is a very special salutation, used only by the prophets Joel, Zechariah, Zephaniah, and then only with reference to the Messiah: "Exult, daughter of Zion, for the Lord is in your midst." At hearing these messianic words addressed to her, and with reference to her alone, her disturbance, which she manifests without knowing it, is spontaneous; but she asks nothing because she is the virgin who listens, who believes, who does not demand an explanation.

A brief aside. Bible scholars are in agreement in telling us that this story does not follow the usual biblical pattern of other miraculous births, for example, when the birth of Isaac was announced to Sarah, or the birth of Samuel to Hannah, or to Zechariah that of the Baptist. These were all events prayed for and desired, made impossible by circumstances of old age or sterility, but for which it was never necessary to ask consent. Instead, the annunciation of Christ's birth follows the biblical pattern of special missions, of extraordinary vocations: there is the initial salutation, the annunciation of a mission, the waiting for a response.

Mary thinks about that messianic salutation, about the evident fact that God was asking something truly great of her. She knows that the Messiah was to be born of a woman (*Protoevangelium*) and that he would be conceived by a virgin of the Hebrew people; she does not know that the woman forechosen is she herself, the humble and unknown daughter of Nazareth. Then the angel explains to her: "Do not be afraid... you will have a son... you will call him Jesus... he will be great, he will be the Son of God, he will be a king...."

Mary does not hesitate for an instant; she seeks no signs, but asks for instructions: how should she act to correspond fully to the will of God? Her question: "How can this be since I know not man?" (in other words, "I have never had conjugal relations"), is an explicit revelation of her proposal of virginity. "Should I continue as I am? Should I change?" She places no conditions on God, she is the handmaid of the Lord; she only asks what she must do. Gabriel's response, "The Holy Spirit will come upon you...," not only explains to her how that Son would be born, nor is it only the confirmation that he will truly be the Son of God; but it also assures her that her proposal of virginity came from God and that it would be maintained also in her marriage.

At this point it is God who awaits a response from his creature. He has created us intelligent and free, and he treats us as such. Even his most exalted gifts are offered to us by the Lord; he never imposes them on us. The Second Vatican Council will say: "The Father of mercies willed that the Incarnation should be preceded by assent on the part of the predestined mother" (LG 56) and it will add in the same paragraph: "Mary was not a mere passive instrument in the hands of God; rather, she freely cooperated in the work of our salvation through faith and obedience." And immediately she gives her ready response: "Behold the handmaid of the Lord; be it done unto me according to your word." I don't know if one can think of a greater moment in the history of humankind comparable to this when the Word of God became flesh and came to live among us. It all came to pass and he has never abandoned us since: "I am with you even to the end of time."

When Adam and Eve were thrown out of their terrestrial paradise, facing a life of fatigue and death, they did not depart in desperation. God had left them a promise when, condemning the serpent who had tricked them, he said: "I will put enmity between you and the woman, and between your offspring and hers; he will strike at your head" (Gn 3:1). There was still hope: that woman and her son (the seed of Eve) would defeat Satan. But when would this woman come? And when would her son triumph? During the long period of waiting, the messianic promise was made more precise. With Abraham God chose a people from whom would be born the Blessed One. From among the various tribes of Israel, his predilection fell on the tribe of Judah; among the many families of Judah the promise would be fixed on that of David. But when and how would the prophecies be fulfilled?

Behold, finally the woman forechosen and blessed was here. Her parents had called her Mary; the angel Gabriel called her "full of heavenly favors"; she herself would call herself "the handmaid of the Lord." She is the promised woman, the virgin who would give birth to a son. The Hebrew people awaited the Messiah, a man. Never would one have thought that the One sent from God would have been his only begotten Son. It is here that the page of the Annunciation becomes ever more important. For the first time the mystery of the Trinity, about which in the Old Testament there were only a few veiled allusions, appears in all its clarity: the *Father* sends the angel Gabriel, who had already appeared to Daniel for the great messianic prophecies, and some months earlier he had appeared to Zechariah to announce to him the birth of John the Baptist; the *Son* took flesh in the womb of the Virgin, thus uniting to his divine nature a human nature, in the sole person of the Word; the *Holy Spirit* descends upon Mary to bring about that great mystery through which Mary, remaining a virgin, becomes a mother, and the mother of the Son of God.

At this point we can only contemplate the wonderful ways of God and how he fulfills his promises much better than we would ever have been able to desire or dream.

Reflections

About Mary — Her greatness: she is great because she is forechosen; she is great because she believes; she is great because she is available to whatever the Lord asks of her, without any conditions. The three names with which she is identified: Mary, meaning "loved by God," is the first step towards that which God wills to do with her; "overflowing with heavenly favors" (we usually say "full of grace") expresses how much the Lord was working in her; "handmaid of the Lord," is the first just response of a human creature before a divine request. The Trinity that reveals itself and works in her this supreme marvel, the incarnation of the Word, acquires a unique and unrepeatable relationship with her, beyond that of every other relationship with created beings.

About us — These marvels of God did not take place for the purpose of honoring Mary, but for our salvation. We see at once the love of the Most High Trinity for each one of us: Jesus became flesh for us, to save us. In all of this the role of Mary in the divine plan which is being fulfilled, her collaboration with God, and the gratitude which we all owe her is evident.

Two Mothers, Two Sons

"Behold, Elizabeth, your kinswoman, in her old age has also conceived a son, and this is the sixth month for her who was called barren; for nothing will be impossible for God." Thus Gabriel spoke to Mary, announcing that the son to be born of her would be conceived through the working of the Holy Spirit, that is, in a totally miraculous way: He who had made the sterile old womb of Elizabeth fruitful was fully able to render fruitful the young womb of Mary, all the while maintaining her virginity. The Madonna never sought a sign or proof. Why then did the angel give her a sign, and why that sign?

That seems to us very understandable. In the first place he wanted to remind Mary that in her would take place an event that was fully miraculous, of which there had never before been any example, nor would there ever be any such example thereafter: that a virgin would conceive through the working of the Holy Spirit, remaining a virgin before, during and after the birth, in conformity with the choice that Mary had made under divine inspiration. But there was also another motive that the very young mother at once understood: announcing to her the miraculous conception of the Baptist, Gabriel wanted her to understand that there was a strict relationship between these two babies, both of them born under miraculous circumstances, even though diverse, and both of whom had been announced by the same Gabriel who had been sent by the Father. Mary understands that there is a link between the two babies, the Son of God and the child of Elizabeth; a bond of mission, for which the Baptist will be the precursor of Jesus, for whom he would prepare the way.

And so we find Mary rushing to the place where the plan of God was beginning to unfold. The mountain city of Judea, where Elizabeth lived, is commonly identified with Ain Karem, some seven kilometers or approximately five miles from Jerusalem. It was easy to find caravans going to the Holy City which one could join for the journey, certainly in the company of a relative. We doubt that Joseph, her husband, would have been her companion, otherwise he would have already discovered the great mystery hidden within his spouse: it would not explain the surprise he expressed upon Mary's return to Nazareth. A trip of about 170 kilometers (106 miles) would have required five or six days on foot (people used to go by foot, but they were used to walking, something which we have completely lost in our day). And then finally there was the great encounter which we generally refer to with the word *Visitation*. I call it the great encounter because it was not a matter of a private visit between relatives. In the Gospel there is no place for episodes of purely personal value; the Gospel is the preaching of the good news, the proclamation of the salvation brought by God; it is not historiography.

Right away we have here a lesson that the evangelist wanted to impart to us and which has perennial value: from the moment when Mary conceived the Son of God, filled with the Holy Spirit, wherever she went, there is also the presence of Jesus and the Spirit. Just look at what Elizabeth immediately experienced as soon as her very young cousin set foot in her house and greeted her. I have no idea of the timbre of Mary's voice, but I know well the efficacy of her presence. And this is not the only first for Elizabeth who had had many others: she is the first who, in the presence of Mary, is filled with the Holy Spirit; she is the first to exalt Mary on account of her maternity: "Blessed are you among women and blessed is the fruit of your womb!"; she is the first to recognize in Mary the Mother of God, calling her "the mother of my Lord"; she is the first to announce an evangelical beatitude: "Blessed is she who has believed." The Bible is full of beatitudes; it is the book of beatitudes. One has only to think of how many Psalms begin with the words: "Blessed is the one who...." This is true also of the Gospels, which contain more than the eight beatitudes from the Sermon on the Mount, even though these have a particular programmatic value of their own. I imagine that Elizabeth, who uttered one of the first, must have had a good collection of them.

At this point it is clear that the protagonists of this encounter are the babies whose two mothers were carrying them in their wombs. John leaps with joy in the presence of his Lord, fulfilling the prophecy spoken by Gabriel to Zechariah, namely, that the baby would be sanctified even in his mother's womb. And thus Jesus begins his great work of sanctification. He has barely been conceived, but he is not just a clot of blood as some modern pro-abortionists pretend who have no qualms about approving murderous laws legalizing the killing of babies in their mothers' wombs; he is the Son of God! This is a lesson that every woman who conceives a child should always bear clearly in mind.

There is also another aspect that needs to be underscored in this marvelous encounter of such great prophetic and salvific value: it reminds us of the biblical episode that seems to be an anticipation of it. When the Ark of the Covenant, which God took possession of, covering it with a cloud to indicate his very presence, was brought to Jerusalem by King David, it at one point came to a halt. When Uzzah dared to touch it to keep it from tipping over, he died suddenly. King David hesitated for a moment, terrified before the holiness of the Ark, and then made it remain in the house of Obededom for three months, the same period which Mary spent with her cousin. Afterward, when he decided to have it brought definitively to Jerusalem, he felt deeply his own unworthiness and exclaimed: "How can the ark of the Lord come to me?" (2 S 6:9).

This whole episode was a prophetic sign. The true Ark of the Covenant is Mary, to whom the angel had said: "The Spirit of the Lord will come upon you, and the power of the Most High will overshadow you." And Elizabeth, filled by the divine presence, repeats the humble sentiments of David: "Who am I that the mother of my Lord should come to me?" This realization of the plan of God, which from its veiled anticipation in the Old Testament finds its fulfillment in the New, is stupendous.

The Visitation provides us with one of the more joyous episodes in the life of Mary. And there aren't many of them! The exultation of Elizabeth and that of John the Baptist tell us clearly of the joy which the presence of Mary brings, wherever she goes, wherever she is welcomed. This is true because with her there is always the presence of Jesus who gives the grace of salvation, and the presence of the Holy Spirit who enlightens us and helps us understand the great mysteries of God.

Reflections

About Mary — She is the true and enduring Ark of the Covenant, that is, the dwelling place of God; actually she is more, because it is she from whom God assumed our human nature to live in our midst as our brother. To welcome Mary is the way to receive Jesus and the Holy Spirit. The first beatitude of the Gospel, "Blessed is she who has believed" is the beatitude of faith; to it corresponds well the last beatitude proclaimed by the risen Christ to Thomas: "Because you have seen me, you have believed; blessed are those who have not seen and yet believed!" (Jn 20:29). Mary is the model of those who believe without having first seen.

About us — Perhaps we have not yet understood who Mary is; the various firsts of Elizabeth are our help and guide. To delude ourselves into thinking we can have Jesus and the Holy Spirit without going through Mary is not in conformity with the way established by God. Faith, not sensibility, tells us that salvation begins by welcoming Mary.

The Song of Joy

I will not repeat here the *Magnificat* (Lk 1:46-55), but ask the reader to keep it in mind. At the exalting and inspiring salutation of Elizabeth, Mary responds with a canticle of praise to God that constitutes the principal hymn of the New Testament. Those who have the duty or the good habit of reciting the evening prayer of Vespers, never miss repeating the song of the Virgin every day. Elizabeth, inspired by the Spirit, addressed Mary with an amazing greeting which we continually repeat whenever we say the *Hail Mary*; it should not surprise us that the Virgin, more filled with the Holy Spirit than ever and the living temple of the Son of God, would respond with a song of such extraordinary richness.

Let us take into consideration the psychological moment which that very young mother was experiencing. Certainly her heart was beating with joy, for all that the Lord was doing in her, having had to close herself within a discrete silence, not being able to confide in anyone. Finally, seeing that her secret had already been revealed to her cousin, herself overjoyed over the unexpected conception of John the Baptist, she can now burst forth freely in that hymn of praise which she had certainly been forming in her mind and singing with all her heart from the moment the angel of the annunciation left her.

The *Magnificat* has unique characteristics. Each one of its expressions, each word finds an echo in the Old Testament of which

25

we can list more than eighty citations. And still the result is not a stitching together of biblical texts, almost an anthology of citations, but an entirely new canticle which reveals all the freshness and spontaneity of the heart in celebration by the one who composed it. Mary is happy. She is happy because God has chosen her, without looking at her nothingness; she is happy because in her there is Jesus: he is the Son of God, but he is her son too, flesh of her flesh, blood of her blood; she already presses him to her heart and dreams of his eyes, his smile, that face which certainly resembles her own more than any other as Dante says. She is happy because she is with a relative who understands her and before whom she can give full expression to her joy.

The happiness of Mary has a unique origin. It derives everything from what God has done for her. For that reason all praise is addressed to God. Elizabeth praises and blesses Mary; Mary praises and blesses God. At the beginning she takes her cue from the canticle of Hannah, another mother who found herself rejoicing in her motherhood through an extraordinary grace of the Lord, since she had been sterile, and sang her praise of God as she awaited the birth of her son Samuel. Then Mary, with references in her song, briefly passes over all the historical and prophetic books of the Bible; above all she cites the Psalms. And still there is nothing burdensome in this cascade of references, but rather all the spontaneity of a new hymn. How can this be? A secret that all of us are called to discover is the beauty of the Psalms: God himself teaches us the words with which to praise him, words that often also reflect our present situation, the state of soul in which we find ourselves in this moment. The biblical prayers are not only prayers; they are also schools of prayer. Whoever uses them habitually, as Mary certainly did, learns also to turn to God in spontaneous prayer which picks up the concepts, and even the same words of the Bible itself. The Second Vatican Council justly encouraged all the faithful to recite the Divine Office, especially Lauds and Vespers, which make up its principal hours (SC 100).

If then we analyze the *Magnificat*, we can easily ascertain its division into three parts from its very different modes of expression and content. At the beginning the song is strictly personal: the Virgin reflects on how much the Lord has done in her. And still, even if the concepts refer to her personally, they express truths that have universal value. All that God has done in Mary has the purpose of putting into motion the plan of salvation. The Lord has turned his glance on the nothingness of his handmaid. She senses that she is nothing, but a nothing that has been the object of the gratuitous choice of God who has done great things in her, because he alone is great, powerful, holy. It is a clear invitation not to look at and praise her, but to look at and to praise God. What has taken place in her, of an exceptional grandeur, is all the work of God.

And she goes on. Just think of the courage of this young girl who, expecting a child, dares to utter a prophecy about herself, which no one else would have ever risked uttering: "From now on all generations will call me blessed." Without enlightenment from Elizabeth, the only other person present, one would think this to be the vain ranting of a deranged woman. Instead, two thousand years later, we are the witnesses of how this prophecy has come true and continues to come true, with an impressive crescendo, throughout the world every day.

The second part of the *Magnificat* presents an entirely different mode of expression. The very meek Mary, reflecting on the ways of God, uses a language that is almost violent: the proud and their projects will be hurled into nothingness; the powerful will be cast down from their thrones; the rich will find themselves reduced to misery. In recompense the humble will be exalted and the hungry will be filled with every good thing. It is already the proclamation of the revolution of the Sermon on the Mount, the proclamation of the Beatitudes. It is a totally new revolution with respect to the canticles of the Old Testament (I think of Deborah, of Miriam the sister of Moses, of Judith), in which God is exalted for military victories. Here the victory is something altogether different.

In the third part Mary identifies with her people, the people of the Covenant, repository of the grand promise. In particular she cites Abraham, the first of those forechosen and of whom she feels herself to be a daughter. God had sworn: "In you will all the nations of the earth be blessed" (Gn 12:3). Mary sees realized in herself all the promises made by God to Israel through the Fathers, but addressed to the salvation of all humanity.

The past is evoked in light of the future; Israel has been raised up that it might be the repository of the divine promises and developed in view of the coming of the Messiah. Now this mission is over because it has been fulfilled in Mary. From her the Messiah himself and the new People of God will take over.

Reflections

About Mary — Humility never contradicts truth. Mary is aware of the greatness to which she has been raised along with the fact that, personally, she had nothing to pride herself in: all is a gift of God, and he alone is to be praised. It is the only time that Mary speaks much; perhaps she wants to teach us that it is very important to speak with God, to adore him, thank him, refer to him all that we may have of good.

About us — The biblical prayers are prayers and schools of prayer; we learn to make them our own whenever we express ourselves with spontaneous prayers inspired by biblical concepts. We unite ourselves to the chorus of all the generations who praise Mary; but we must never stop at Mary; through her we always arrive at God. *"Per Mariam ad Jesum"*: Through Mary to Jesus. It is for this reason that the worship and the heart of all the Marian sanctuaries is never Mary, but Jesus in the Eucharist.

How a Just Man Suffers

"Now the birth of Jesus came about in the following manner: When his mother Mary was betrothed to Joseph, but before they came together, she was found to be with child by the Holy Spirit. Joseph her husband was a good and upright man so he was planning to put her away, but quietly because he didn't wish to disgrace her. But while he was thinking these things over, behold, an angel of the Lord appeared to him in a dream and said, 'Joseph son of David, don't be afraid to take your wife Mary into your house — the child who has been conceived in her is from the Holy Spirit. She'll give birth to a son and you shall name him Jesus, because he'll save his people from their sins'" (Mt 1:18-21).

Let us note how meticulously Matthew narrates these facts. It is very important to know with precision how the things came about, not to satisfy our historical interest which, as we have already pointed out, departs from the intentions of the evangelists, but to confirm us in the truths which are of fundamental salvific importance: that Jesus is truly the Son of God, conceived by the working of the Holy Spirit, as Luke has told us in the page of the Annunciation; and that Jesus is truly the promised Messiah in whom all the prophecies have been realized. In particular: that he was to be a descendant of David and that he would be conceived by a virgin. These are the things that Matthew wants to establish, for which he takes as a starting point a fact that was becoming ever more evident following the three months that Mary had spent with Elizabeth: Joseph noticed that his wife was with child.

What dramatic days of atrocious doubts that young husband must have spent! A just man, he had decided to enter into a holy marriage in conformity with the law of Moses. And he had contracted marriage with the certainty of having found an ideal spouse: a girl whom he knew from her birth (in that little village this was true for everyone), toward whom he had immense esteem and affection such as to absolutely exclude the possibility of his being faced with betrayal. If he had thought that, he would have had the duty to denounce his wife for being unfaithful. Perhaps parents and friends were already rejoicing with him over the child who was to be born; in Joseph there was only torment that would not give him peace, which grew from week to week, as did the sorrowful decision which was maturing in him.

We are surprised at Mary's silence. But if we think about her personality, her way of comporting herself, it no longer surprises us, and we find that her silence followed the most reasonable way of behaving in this occasion. Even she must have suffered tremendous pain. She read in the eyes of her spouse — ever more noticeable with every encounter — the doubt, the suffering, the uncertainty about what he should do, but she knew that it was not up to her to intervene. What was taking place in her was extraordinary and was the fulfillment of a greater divine plan. It was not her duty to reveal it and to make him understand; a fact so extraordinary belonged to the Father who had sent the angel to her; to the Son whom she carried in her womb; to the Spirit who had made her fruitful. And so she kept quiet and waited, when keeping quiet and waiting were the two things that cost her the most. We admire Mary's silence but the silence of God bewilders us. With Elizabeth the sound of Mary's voice was enough because the Spirit revealed everything. How much Joseph must have suffered because of Mary's silence, but how much Mary must have suffered because of the silence of God.

Little by little Joseph reached the most sorrowful decision of all. He was convinced that he found himself facing a mystery, an event too great for him to comprehend. It would be better to call a halt to everything. In the most delicate way possible, "in secret" as Matthew tells us (only two witnesses were required), he decided to give his wife a decree of divorce. In those days it was very easy for a husband to repudiate his own wife, under any kind of pretext. And the bill of divorce was considered a guarantee for the woman who was then free to remarry. Only when Joseph in his suffering had reached this decision, did the angel, all alone, arrive on the scene to reveal the truth to him. Let's be honest. Aren't we immediately inclined to ask: Why didn't God send the angel earlier? Why did he allow so much time of piercing sorrow for both holy spouses, so loved and precious to him, to pass? I believe that they were the same motives for which the Father asked of his Son the sacrifice of the cross. The ways of God are not our own. The Lord asks us to do his will. He does not ask us to understand the profound motives behind it which are often superior to our earthly capacity to grasp.

At this point we can understand Joseph's joy. "Do not be afraid to take Mary your wife into your house," the angel said. He was no longer afraid; he will run to Mary with all the strength he had left, to tell her that now he knows everything, that all is clear. He would want to set the day for their solemn nuptials as soon as possible. After so much fear of having to separate from his beloved spouse, now he felt certain that he would never again be separated from her. For the Virgin, too, it will be the end of a nightmare and she will have thanked God who had rewarded her faith, her abandonment, in this way.

But these are only personal, human considerations. What Joseph understood is another thing entirely. He understood that his spouse was above all things the Mother of God. He understood that he was the fortunate descendant of David, through whom the messianic prophecies were to be fulfilled. He understood that his marriage to Mary was completely different from what he had imagined it would be: God entrusted to him the dearest and most precious persons who ever existed: Jesus and Mary. He understood and accepted with gratitude his role, of which he will feel totally unworthy. Here we truly have to discover the plan of God with regard to the figure of Joseph; we will speak of it in our next reflection.

In conclusion let us limit ourselves to noting how the prophecy of Isaiah, "A virgin shall conceive," receives a precise explanation only in Matthew. Often the prophecies of the Old Testament contain veiled hints which are clarified only at the moment of their realization. Even in this case the expression is not clear. The same term used by Isaiah, *almah*, could indicate a girl, a young spouse. Only through the extraordinary maternity of Mary and the reminder of Matthew are we able to understand the exact sense: a virgin.

Reflections

About Mary — Her divine maternity did not exempt her from suffering. Perhaps Joseph's doubt and the uncertainty regarding his decision, was the first of her great sufferings; but there will be others much greater and continual in the future. St. Teresa of Avila rightly notes that the Lord sends more crosses to those he loves the most. His election of the Blessed Virgin Mary did not give her an understanding of the plan of God which would preserve her from doubts, uncertainty, or questions which went without an answer.

About us — Often the path of our life follows a course completely different from what we had foreseen. Joseph for us is a great model of availability. The Lord is not bound to give us an explanation of his behavior. He seeks those who will do his will, even if often he says nothing to them or does not enable them to comprehend his motives. At times he asks for an active intervention; at other times he asks a trusting abandonment. To have patience, to be quiet, to wait, are virtues which often cost us more than to act.

Happy Spouses United by God

"Do not be afraid to take Mary your wife into your house." Because this was Joseph's greatest desire, in all his suffering he feared most having to renounce his wife. Once every doubt had been happily resolved, there was nothing left to do but to proceed with the solemn nuptials, that is, to the introduction of his wife into her new home which in the meantime he had prepared. Even the poor, for that unique occasion in their lives, with the help of their parents, took pains to solemnize the feast to the maximum. Thus it is easy to presume that even the wedding of Joseph and Mary was a very happy one, with the presence of many relatives and friends, enlivened by music and song throughout the seven days as was customary in those times.

But between the two spouses there was a secret known to them alone: there was the presence of the Son of God who had brought them together and for whom they would live their lives. For this reason Joseph could not have been unaware of the sacredness of that gesture of introducing Mary, the new and true Ark of God, into his home. It is easy enough to imagine, with the knowledge that all Jews have of the Bible, that he would have thought of the sacred passage: "In those days David assembled all Israel in Jerusalem to bring the Ark of the Lord to the place which he had prepared for it.... He commanded the chiefs of the Levites to appoint their brethren as chanters, to play on musical instruments, harps, lyres, and cymbals, to make a loud sound of rejoicing" (1 Ch 15:3ff).

But there is still a little more. We have yet to confront another argument which helps us to appreciate the greatness of Joseph for the role which God entrusted to him and which he accepted with joy. Conscious of his littleness, he, too, would have uttered the words of David and Elizabeth before the Ark of the Covenant and the true Ark of God: "Who am I, that the mother of my Lord — and my Lord himself — should come to my house?" He was beginning to be aware of certain things which helped him to understand his role.

One sure reason for which he had been chosen, a reason mentioned by the angel in the annunciation to Mary and by the angel who appeared to him in a dream: he was a son of David, a member of the house of David; and it is through him, by reason of his marriage to Mary, that the Messiah would fulfill the prophecy of his belonging to the family of David. It may seem very little to us; it might even seem better to us had Mary belonged to the house of David. Instead it was not to be. We must remember that often the messianic prophecies are generic and that God in fulfilling them takes great liberties. From the beginning, when the prophet Nathan promised David an enduring house (2 S 7:14), it was natural to think of a royal dynasty lasting for an indeterminate period of time. Instead, the Davidic dynasty ended with the deportation to Babylon. Upon their return from exile, the sole important personage among the descendants of David is Zerubbabel; but he lived nearly five hundred years before Christ. From then on the house of David no longer had any political importance, and the words of Nathan came to always be interpreted in a messianic sense. God fulfilled them through the marriage of Mary and Joseph.

But Joseph understood something far more important: he understood who his spouse was and who the baby she had conceived truly was. Mary was the long awaited woman prophesied in Genesis; she was the virgin mother predicted by Isaiah as a sign of salvation; the son, conceived by the working of the Holy Spirit, was the very Son of God himself, who had God as his Father. He understood that the silence of Mary served a dual purpose: to safeguard the secret of the identity of that child, a secret which Jesus himself would reveal little by little and with great discretion; and she was silent in order not to reveal her personal identity as Mother of God.

I believe that this is the moment in which Joseph seriously reflected on himself, realizing how much God must have expected of him by entrusting Jesus and Mary to him. If at first he had such an esteem of Mary as to exclude in every way any thought of infidelity on her part, now this esteem was transformed into true veneration: Joseph is truly the first great devotee of Mary most holy. But there is more. In the first centuries of Christianity the figure of Joseph was studied and known better than it is today. I think, for example, of the great ark covered with mosaics in the church of Santa Maria Maggiore in Rome, dating back to the year 432 in remembrance of that day in Ephesus when Mary was proclaimed Mother of God. Observing the various scenes, we see that Joseph stands out in four of them: he is seen as the head of the Holy Family and of the Church, representative of the bishop, witness and custodian of the virginity of Mary, protector and educator of Jesus.

Regarding Jesus himself, the secret which Joseph along with Mary kept in their hearts, is the divine identity of their son. But the secret also involved the mission of that child which the angel had revealed to him in the words: "You will name him Jesus for he will save his people from their sins." These words defined the work for which the Son of God became man: to save, to redeem from sin, and thus to reopen the gates of heaven. Joseph himself would be in charge of the human formation and education of the Son of God in order to prepare him for his mission.

At this point it is not difficult to understand the joyful "Yes" of Joseph, so like the joyful *fiat* of Mary, at the role which the Father had given him. His marriage would be different from what he had imagined and looked forward to, but it was to be immensely greater. When God calls someone to an extraordinary mission, he always asks the renunciation of their human plans and ways of looking at things. He did so with Abraham when he invited him to leave his house and homeland and to start off, without telling him where he would lead him. So it was with the prophets (it's enough to think of Amos) who expected simply to carry on the work of their fathers; so it happened with the apostles, when he invited them to leave all to follow him. And thus he continues to do with whomever he calls to a total dedication to him.

When, on December 8, 1870, Pope Pius IX proclaimed St. Joseph patron of the universal Church, it seemed to many that he was invoking one protector too many at a time in which the temporal power of the popes was coming to an end. It was rather the recognition of an evangelical fact: by entrusting the person of Jesus to Joseph, God also entrusted to him his mystical body, the Church.

Reflections

About Mary — Her trust, her abandonment in God, received full recompense even if it came after much sorrow. From that moment Mary also had the assistance of a most faithful companion who would share with her her joys and sorrows, as she would share with him the secrets of her own identity and that of Jesus. The relationship between Mary and Joseph, from the moment that their union was willed by God for taking care of Jesus, was one of extreme respect and understanding. There were no conjugal relations, but there was true love, that love which is not confined to the senses.

About us — Availability to God's plans, expressed through our gifts and the circumstances of our lives, can often bring us to have to renounce certain projects and goals. The plan of God for each one of us is always a plan of salvation: so long as we remain in the will of God, our life will be a success in whatever case. And beside the help of Mary, we invoke the help of Joseph, feeling ourselves entrusted to him as a member of the body of Christ.

Bethlehem, House of Bread

"Now it happened that in those days a decree went out from Caesar Augustus that all the world should be registered." Thus Luke (2:1) introduces us to the grand event of the Nativity. God makes use of secondary causes which seem to us wholly accidental in order to accomplish his designs. The prophet Micah had prophesied that the Messiah would be born in Bethlehem; the Lord made use of this circumstance so that Jesus would be born precisely there.

Bethlehem, which means "House of Bread" (the Eucharistic implication does not elude us), was a tiny village some seven kilometers (about 4.5 miles) from Jerusalem. Now it is a small growing town in ongoing development that has almost joined the larger city. We find Bethlehem mentioned several times in the Bible. Naomi departed from there with her two married sons who died without leaving heirs. Naomi returned to Bethlehem, her birthplace, accompanied by one of her daughters-in-law, the Moabite Ruth. The biblical account in the book which takes its name from Ruth, tells us with admiration of the providential choice this foreigner made. Invited by Naomi to go back to her own home, as the other daughter-in-law had done, Ruth makes a courageous and faith-filled choice: "Your people will be my people, and your God will be my God." She will marry Boaz and will merit being part of the genealogy of the Messiah, becoming the great-grandmother of David. At Bethlehem, in the presence of his brothers, David will be anointed king by Samuel while Saul was still ruling.

These are big events for so small a place. But the greatest event of all, which will render Bethlehem known throughout the world, will be the birth of Jesus.

Joseph was accompanied by Mary on the occasion of the census. Note that women were not obliged to have their names inscribed; perhaps Joseph did not want to leave Mary so close to her giving birth, or perhaps he wanted Mary to be inscribed in the census among the members of the family of David so that the baby too would be considered fully a member of such a family. "But there was no room for them in the inn." I think that the provisional choice of the newlyweds must have been dictated by convenience, taking into account the event which was about to take place in Mary. Certainly relatives, so hospitable among the Jews, would have taken them in. But the homes consisted of a single room wherein at night they spread some mats and all slept on the floor together. It was not a good solution. In the caravan, there were some quiet rooms, but for a price and hence not convenient for the poor. Or you could sleep under the porticoes with all the others; but even this was hardly a satisfactory solution. Better, then, was an isolated cave which served as an occasional refuge for shepherds and their flocks. There was such a shelter near at hand, poor but discrete and peaceful. And it is here, we would say in wretched conditions, that Jesus was born. And still what natural majesty there was in his surroundings! Even today, contemplating Bethlehem from the "shepherds' field," especially at the hour of sunset or during the night, one remains enchanted by the hilly countryside, the vegetation, the crystal clear sky. Above all Jesus was welcomed by the two purest hearts in the world. Byzantine Catholics express all this with a beautiful Christmas prayer: "What shall we offer you, O Christ, for having appeared on earth as a man? Each one of the creatures created by you offer you in fact their appreciation; the angels, their song; the heavens, a star; the magi, their gifts; the shepherds, their admiration; the earth, a grotto; the desert, a manger. But we offer you as your mother the Virgin Mary."

St. Francis, with his poetic sensibility, wanted to reproduce a live replica of the Nativity and in this way he so spread the popularity of the crib that, on Christmas day, we see them everywhere: in churches, homes, oftentimes in plazas, on the streets, and in shop windows. And we repeat with confidence, in the midst of all those concerns which so preoccupy us, the consoling words of Isaiah: "A child is born to us, a son is given us," the Son of God.

More than ever at Christmas Mary shines on account of her most high elevation as Mother of God. But we have to understand well the meaning of this stupendous title. We never read this expression in the Gospel, for in them Mary is always shown and called "the mother of Jesus." But it is just as clearly said in the Gospels that Jesus is God. For that reason, when the first Christian writers used the term *Theotókos* (begetter of God) they encountered no objections. It was Nestorius who opposed this title because he had fallen into a Christological error; he held that in Jesus there were two persons, one divine and the other human. According to him, Mary was the mother only of the human person of Christ; she was the mother of a man. A polemic arose which the Council of Ephesus settled in 431. The main preoccupation of the Council was Christological: it defined that in Jesus there is one person only, that of the Word who, taking flesh in Mary, united to his divine nature a human nature. As a consequence Mary is truly the Mother of God because her Son is truly God.

It is important that we understand this truth so as not to fall into error ourselves. Never is it to be understood in such a way as to make of Mary a goddess. She remains always a humble creature like ourselves, who had need of being redeemed by Christ. Nor does that title signify that God had need of a mother in order to give him his divinity. The title "Mother of God" is a Christological title: it means that Jesus, born of Mary, is true God. With that title we affirm that Jesus is God from the very first moment of his conception. Therefore Mary is truly the mother of a Son who is God. And it is for this reason that we proclaim her Mother of God.

For us as Catholics these concepts are clear. We must, however, also know how to express them with precision, to respond to any eventual objections. Let us add that, for the most part, even for the Orthodox and for the Protestants there was never much doubt concerning these two Marian dogmas, defined from of old, before the split: viz., that Mary is the Mother of God and ever virgin. The difficulties, especially for some confessions of the Protestant Reform, have had to do with the two latest Marian dogmas of more recent promulgation: the Immaculate Conception and the Assumption. Towards these truths they have various positions; some confessions propose them as a possibility which one is free to believe or not. But perhaps the greatest difficulty is given by other Marian titles which we attribute to the Virgin and have developed into a cult.

Reflections

About Mary — Certainly the day of Jesus' birth was one of the most joyful days of her life, and hence she probably did not feel the inconvenience of the makeshift arrangements. Mary's greatness as Mother of God did not take away her humility, her ability to give credit for everything to the gratuitous gift of God. In this she is more appealing to us than ever in her maternity.

About us — Let us think of the joy of Christmas in a religious sense: to thank the Father, to adore the Son, to open ourselves to the inspirations of the Holy Spirit. We can reflect on our own welcome of God made man. It is important to know how to view his coming with humility in order to understand that he came to save us, to redeem us. When he will return in the splendor of his glory, he will come to judge the living and the dead and to give to each one what he or she has earned. Let us entrust ourselves to the Mother of God that she may help us to know the Son of God and her son ever more.

The Faith of the Little Ones

God has an unquestionable predilection for the little ones, the poor, persons who, in the judgment of the world, count for nothing. It was only right that the first announcement of the birth of the Messiah would be given to the Hebrew people, and this is one of the most significant elements of the entire episode. But it also reveals to us God's taste in his choice of those who would be so privileged. Shepherds back then did not enjoy a good reputation, notwithstanding the importance of herding sheep in the overall economy of Israel. It's enough to know that they could not be elected judges, nor could they give witness in a trial. We would say that they lacked full civil rights. But it was precisely to them that God sent the angelic revelation with these words: "Behold I bring you good news which will give joy to the whole nation, because this day in the city of David a Savior has been born for you who is the Messiah, the Lord. And this will be the sign for you — you will find a baby, swaddled and lying in a manger" (Lk 2:10-12).

Isaiah had prophesied that among the messianic signs the good news would be preached to the poor. Here we have its first realization. The poor are immediately ready to believe and prompt to move. The sign of recognition is extremely indicative, it is not something generic as it might seem to us. Other than pointing out to them the human poverty of the child, it helps them find him. Even in the poorest of families, when a mother was expecting a baby, a little basket or crib would be prepared in which to place it. That an infant might be placed in a manger signified not only that it was poor, but that it belonged to persons who were merely passing through. Once the shepherds had arrived in Bethlehem, it would not have been difficult for them to find out if anyone had seen a traveler about to give birth and to be given directions to where they might have taken refuge.

The shepherds saw and believed. They saw a crying infant and believed that he was the promised Messiah. Overjoyed at this they are the first to proclaim the Christ, to announce the good news that the Savior had been born. They speak very simply of what they had heard from the angels and of what they had seen, without fear or human respect. They didn't even consider the problem of whether they would be believed or ridiculed. To them it was enough that they bear witness to the fact. It is from them that we learn the wondrous song of the angels: "Glory to God in the highest and on earth peace to those he loves." That song will never cease to be a part of our liturgy, nor will the shepherds, in their representation in our manger scenes, ever be forgotten. The angelic words almost seem programmatic, they are a kind of summary of the work of Christ, come to give glory to God and bring peace to humankind. These two immense goals are strictly linked: only giving glory to God and observing his laws can bring peace to the heart of each one and to society as a whole. When people acknowledge God as Father, they become aware that they are brothers and sisters to one another and will live as such.

The episode of the visit of the shepherds concludes with a phrase that is somewhat mysterious, which Luke repeats also at the conclusion of the finding of Jesus in the Temple when he was twelve years old. It seems that he wants to tell us that the heart of Mary is the blackboard on which she kept all these memories: "Mary, for her part, remembered all this and pondered it in her heart" (Lk 2:19). It is an affirmation of the wise meditation that Mary made of the various episodes in the life of her son; but it also seems that the evangelist wants to reveal to us what the source of his information had been. Let us not forget that Luke, at the beginning of his Gospel, states that he was writing of the events "just as those who were *eyewitnesses* and ministers of the word from the beginning have handed them down to us," and he insists on this, adding that he had decided to write "after carefully examining everything *from the beginning*."

We are happy to insist on these passages, because it is very important to know what the source of Luke's information was, not only with regard to the episode of the shepherds, but also as regards all that part which we call the "Infancy Gospel," that is as regards what we have been discussing. The recalling of eyewitnesses (he is not content with indirect testimony) and his careful examination of everything going back to the beginning, substantiates what the Fathers and the exegetes long held, viz., that Luke's source of information was the Virgin Mary herself.

Here it gives me great pleasure to sum up, in this regard, what a contemporary biblical scholar, Aristide Serra, professor at the Pontifical University "Marianum" writes. He affirms that: (1) In the bosom of the first apostolic community Mary was the sole "eye-witness" of the incarnation and of the years of the private life of Jesus; while many were the witnesses to his public life. (2) Pentecost enabled everyone, besides being able to understand fully, to "witness" what they had seen and heard, even if not all were called to "evangelize." Moreover Mary shows, in her *Magnificat*, that she was fully conscious of the marvelous things which God was doing in her. From this, therefore, rose the obligation, so inculcated in her from the Old Testament, to make other generations aware of the wonderful works of God. (3) With these premises it does not seem possible to imagine that the Virgin would have remained silent, closed in upon herself, jealous of the divine mysteries of which she was the protagonist. It is logical to suppose instead that she would have poured out on the Church the treasures which she kept in her heart and which they did not possess. For this reason it is only right to imagine that Mary was always ready "to witness" to the facts to the apostles and to those who, in order to teach or to write, had recourse to her as to a unique and secure source. We know that Luke belonged to the latter.

It doesn't surprise us, after all that Luke wrote about the Virgin, that a tradition would have sprung up around him as "Mary's painter." In various churches Marian images which bear the title of "The Madonna of St. Luke" are venerated. These are simply icons of the type known as "*Odigitria*" (lit., she who shows us the way; Guide of Wayfarers). The most ancient of these goes back to the sixth century; the most famous to the twelfth and thirteenth centuries. It is clear that these are not the "paintings" of St. Luke except insofar as he "depicted in words" the principal facts of her life.

Reflections

About Mary — She is the first to be named when the shepherds approach the grotto. It seems that she is the first to present Jesus, thus initiating his precious mission: the child born of her is not for her; it is for the Father and for humanity. Far from watching over him possessively, she presents him, offers him, collaborates with him from the very beginning of his mission.

About us — It is necessary for us to make ourselves little, to "become like little children," in order to understand the secrets of God. That requires an openness of soul, a humility, which enables everything. The life of the Church also presents us with many persons of culture, persons who hold posts of great prestige and responsibility, even kings or princes, persons who were blessed with that humility of heart and total availability to God, such as to be able to comprehend and live his teaching. The shepherds see and witness; Mary knows and does not hesitate to reveal the grandeur of God. All Christians ought to feel within themselves the duty to bear witness to the faith which animates them.

The Name of Salvation

"And when eight days had passed for his circumcision, they gave him the name Jesus, the name given him by the angel before he was conceived in his mother's womb" (Lk 2:21). Circumcision, practiced by other peoples as well, became a sacred rite with Abraham when God imposed it on him as a sign of belonging to the Chosen People. It obligated the one receiving it to the observance of the law given by God and was not a mere formality, a mere external sign: the prophets always and often spoke of a "circumcision of the heart," that is, an opening of the soul to the love of God and neighbor. Today, to belong to the People of God, Jesus instituted Baptism, in which the promises which sum up the principal duties of the Christian are pronounced.

Jesus, too, observed this rite which was normally performed at home by the father or another apt person. And from that moment on, he officially belonged to the Hebrew people, a membership which was never contested by anyone. A rite and a name: from then on salvation no longer depended on that rite, but on that name. A name had great importance to the Jews: for relatives who had the same name and for the biblical figures which they recalled. When a name was imposed from heaven, then, or changed by the will of God, it acquired even greater importance, because it indicated the mission willed by the Father.

"Jesus" means "Savior." "He will save his people from their

sins," the angel had said to Joseph. It is a new mission inasmuch as the people were expecting a Great Prophet; they were hoping for liberation from the Romans and political greatness. Instead, what they received was infinitely greater. Jesus had come to destroy the works of Satan, as St. John affirms; he came to free all those who found themselves under the yoke of the devil, as St Peter said to Cornelius. His is the name of salvation and grace. We are reminded of a few evangelical texts: "All that you ask the Father in my name, he will give you"; "In my name you will cast out demons and heal the sick"; "Whoever gives a mere glass of water in my name will not go without his reward." Peter and John when they performed the first miracle in the name of Jesus, healing a paralytic who was begging at the gate of the Temple, proclaimed in a loud voice: "It is through faith in the name of Jesus that this man whom you see and know has been strengthened, and faith in that name has given him his health in full view of all of you. For no other name under heaven has been given to us by which we may be saved" (cfr. Ac 3 and 4).

Everywhere he went, the great preacher St. Bernardine of Siena distributed leaflets and signs to attach to the doors of one's house or to have engraved on the molding above the door bearing the image of the radiating sun in which were written three letters: JHS "*Jesus Hominum Salvator*," Jesus Savior of Humankind. When he preached in a city, he wanted every family to put this sign on their front door to remind them of the name that saves. We understand very well that the name of Jesus has extraordinary power, but it is not a magic word. The power comes from the faith of the one who invokes the person of the Lord and calls upon him in that name which indicates his mission, having been made flesh "for us men and for our salvation" as we repeat in the Creed. Those who believe that they can obtain some effect by calling on the name of Jesus mechanically, without a profound faith in the divine person, will not obtain anything.

But the episode on which we are reflecting contains yet another truth of exceptional importance. In this singular occasion, in which the circumcision took place (membership in the Jewish people) and the imposition of the name of Jesus (he who saves), a new reality is coming into being, turning everything upside down, an authentic break. From that moment on salvation no longer depends on circumcision but on the name of Jesus. Today we find it hard to comprehend the almost tragic difficulty in which the first Christians who were pious Jews, and very observant ones at that, came to find themselves. They continued to go to the Temple every day and to very faithfully observe the laws which God had given to their forefathers. But the difficulty arose when pagans began to be converted and it exploded in all its crudeness when Paul and Barnabas began to preach with so much success to the Gentiles. Here then is the problem: Did these converts have to submit to circumcision or not? Notice that circumcision brought with it also the obligation to observe in all its details the law given to the Chosen People.

It was the first great difficulty confronted in apostolic times. Later on it will be said: the world was ready to become Christian, but it would never have accepted to become Jewish. Paul saw the gravity of the danger when he began to preach that circumcision no longer had any value, because salvation depended on faith in Jesus Christ. He was hotly contested everywhere he went by the Jewish Christians, that is, by those Christians who had come over from Judaism. The matter was referred to the apostles in Jerusalem: it is the so-called First Council. There was a hot debate. We have to take into account the mentality of those Jews who had become Christians: they saw in the faith of their Fathers the promises which were fulfilled in Jesus who was a Jew, circumcised, observant of the law, even if he did place emphasis, not on the letter of the law but on its substance. And we must understand the theological difficulty: if circumcision was necessary, salvation which depended solely on faith in Jesus Christ would be negated. Further, it would shut off, in one blow, the evangelization to all peoples. The apostles, enlightened by the Holy Spirit, said that Paul was right: no more circumcision, it no longer served.

Thus the definitive break between the Synagogue and the Church came about: we are saved by faith in Jesus Christ, the one who reconciles in himself the people of the Old Covenant and the new People of God. Later on the Church knew other analogous problems, even if not so tragic as that first dilemma; problems nonetheless which, poorly understood and poorly resolved, blocked the evangelization of the world. One thinks, for example, of the incomprehension of the Chinese and Malabar Rite Christians at the time of Benedict XIV. There were times in which it seemed that it was necessary to become Western in order to become Christian. The decisive opening, even if still not total, took place at the Second Vatican Council, especially in *Gaudium et spes*, where respect for all cultures, in which it is necessary to value all that is compatible with Christianity, is proclaimed.

Reflections

About Mary — At his circumcision, the Virgin saw the first blood spilled by her son and his first suffering, and perhaps she saw in it something prophetic. She had the joy of calling Jesus by his name, signifying that mission of which she had already benefitted in anticipation. She also understood that that name would resound in benediction for all the earth.

About us — Let us reflect on our Baptism, given by the will of Jesus in the name of the Trinity, which makes us members of the new People of God, participants in the divine nature, members of Christ, united to his priestly, prophetic and kingly mission, and which confers on us the Holy Spirit. Let us invoke the name of Jesus with faith, deepening our appreciation of its power.

Jesus Is Offered to the Father

Through Moses God ordered that all firstborn children be redeemed because they belonged to him. It was a reminder of the tenth and last plague of Egypt in which all the firstborn of the Egyptians were exterminated while those of the Hebrews were spared. It was the culminating episode that made Pharaoh decide to let the Chosen People go.

At the time of Christ, it was enough to send to the Temple an offering of five silver shekels, equaling approximately two months' wages for the average worker. It was also necessary to send two animals (for the poor two pigeon doves sufficed), one for the holocaust and one for the purification that all women were obliged to undergo. When the firstborn was a male, all of this took place forty days after his birth.

Luke very much wanted to emphasize that everything the young couple did was done in order to comply with the law of Moses. But he actually describes the comportment of Mary and Joseph in such unique detail that we cannot fail to see how they fulfilled in full that rite which had been mandated in a way that veiled the reality fulfilled only with Jesus. First of all it was not prescribed that the couple go to the Temple. This fact, even given the nearness of Bethlehem to Jerusalem, which made this unrequired homage easier to accomplish, already tells us that they went beyond the call of duty.

We find no other such example in the Bible. Then Luke speaks of "*their* purification," seeming to include Joseph. Even this detail reveals a more profound purpose. The saintly couple, undoubtedly moved by divine inspiration, truly offered that son to the Father who was his true Father from every point of view. And it is already evident that he is a sin offering, an offering for the remission of sins, as is his mission. For this reason Luke includes both Joseph and Mary. The two spouses will serve as the representatives of all the people, that the offering of Jesus might take place in the context of a purification.

The value of this episode is prophetic. Let us not forget that, for Luke, Jerusalem is always seen as the city of the passion. Here we note that the rite of the mother's purification has no value whatsoever; instead the offering of her son has enormous importance: it is a true sacrificial offering, to which Mary associates herself understanding its significance even if she would have understood only vaguely that it was a foretelling in anticipation of an entirely different offering, that of the cross. The cross will be the salvation of all humanity. It is interesting to note that, in this passage, Jesus is already proclaimed the "light to the Gentiles."

In fact, at this point a detail is introduced into the narrative that completes and fully explains the sacrificial offering that has just taken place: the encounter with the aged Simeon. This pious Israelite had received a promise from the Holy Spirit: "You will not die without first having seen the Messiah." It is the Spirit who inspires him to go to the Temple on that day and it is the Spirit who, in the midst of the usual comings and goings of the Temple, causes him to approach the young couple. He addresses the mother who is taken by surprise to ask a favor of her: he wants to take the baby in his arms, he wants to look closely at him, to pronounce a stupendous prayer which will let the holy couple know that the Lord had revealed to him the true identity of that child. It is a prayer that is repeated every evening by those who recite Compline or Night Prayer, and it can be summarized in this way: "Now, O Lord, you can take me to yourself in peace because you have given me the joy of seeing the Savior as you promised." Then he exalts the baby, calling him the "light of the Gentiles" and the "glory of Israel."

But at this point the meeting with the saintly old man takes another turn. The face of Simeon may well have darkened as he directly addressed the mother, the true mother, with a double and sorrowful prophecy: one for the baby and one for herself who would be so closely and fully associated with the mission of her son. Who knows how his heavy words must have fallen on the heart of Mary: "He is destined to bring about the fall and rise of many in Israel and to be a sign that will be opposed." His were dreadful words which weigh on each one of us who will be judged on the basis of our acceptance or refusal of Jesus and his teachings. On our response and our coherent behavior will depend whether Jesus will be for us salvation or ruin. No less grave are the prophetic words addressed to the mother: "And a sword shall pierce your own soul, so that the thoughts of many hearts may be revealed."

The prophecy regarding Jesus shows clearly that no one can remain indifferent before his person. He himself will say: "Whoever is not with me is against me." Here on earth we delude ourselves if we think we can more or less assume this attitude: "Lord, I have nothing against you, I respect you, but leave me in peace; that way we will both be OK." As if we did not totally depend on God, "in whom we live and move and have our being," as St. Paul stated in his discourse to the Athenians. As if we had not been created by God in view of Christ and for Christ; because of whom, if the Lord did not sustain us, we would immediately fall into nothingness. As if we could treat God as an equal, imposing our conditions on him.

It is more difficult to explain the prophecy regarding Mary. Why is it necessary that a sword pierce her heart, that is to rend and divide her whole life, in order to reveal the most intimate thoughts of the hearts of men? We see in these words a union between the sufferings of Mary and the sufferings of her son, and a hint of the final separation which will take place at the judgment.

At this point, with Joseph and Mary being in a state of wonder, the presence of the elderly Anna — also full of the Holy Spirit, showing that she had also received full enlightenment regarding the true identity of Jesus for which she praises the Lord and speaks of the baby, pointing him out as the Savior of all those who were waiting for the redemption of Jerusalem — must have come as a welcome balm. She speaks to the little ones, to those who have a heart open to the designs of God and await their unfolding with confidence.

Reflections

About Mary — More than ever we see her in the posture of offering: she offers not only herself, but she offers the son which is hers, but which is not for her. She offers him to the Father for the salvation of humankind from their sins. The wonder with which, together with Joseph, she assists at these events, tells us how the Lord is preparing her little by little, by means of the difficult walk of faith. The prophecy about Jesus is twofold: it is one of joy and one of sorrow. But the prophecy regarding her is only a promise of continual suffering.

About us — Let us offer ourselves to the Father that he might fulfill his designs in us. Take a decisive position with regard to Christ: Who is Jesus for me? How can I seek to know him that I might be able to obey him? Am I aware that his sacrificial suffering is for my salvation, but that it depends on me whether or not it is applied to me for my redemption? The figure of Joseph seems shadowy in this episode. And still, in the presence of the protagonists, it is he who best represents us: he takes part and receives the fruits of the redemption.

Homage from Pagans

Matthew tells us about the Magi's visit to the baby. These wise men, hailing from the East, most probably from Arabia, were experts in astronomy, a much studied science from ancient times. It is interesting to see how God adapts himself to diverse customs and mentalities: to notify the shepherds that Jesus had been born, since he was dealing with Hebrews who well knew from the Bible of the existence of angels, he made use of these celestial messengers. To notify these pagan wise men, instead, he made use of signs conformed to their understanding; an extraordinary star, certainly miraculous, to indicate a prodigious event and able even to indicate the home of the Holy Family. Hence it can hardly be identified with a comet or any of the celestial stars known to us.

We can place this episode a little more than a year after the birth of Jesus. We deduce this from the fact that Herod, calculating the time of the appearance of the star, allowing for a certain margin of safety, had all the baby boys under two years of age slaughtered. We are used to placing the statuettes of the Magi in our nativity scenes because Epiphany falls so close to Christmas and it is convenient to make use of the already prepared crib. But the Gospel tells us that the Magi found the baby and his mother "in the house." It is most probable that the provisional use of the cave lasted for a very short time, perhaps only the forty days in which the mother was not to leave the house after giving birth. In the meantime Joseph would have been looking for a more convenient arrangement and would have gone back to his work. One can imagine that he would have wanted to avoid putting the newborn through the travail of the return trip to Nazareth. And it is also easy to suppose that he must have been able to make very satisfactory arrangements, both with respect to a house as to his work inasmuch as, upon his return from Egypt, his first plan was to go back to Bethlehem.

The salvific importance of this visit has always been recognized in this fact: as Jesus revealed himself to the Hebrews in the persons of the shepherds, so now he reveals himself to the pagans in the persons of the Magi. The gifts have a symbolic value which tradition explains in this fashion: with gold the royalty of Christ is recognized, with incense homage is paid to his divinity, and the myrrh foretells his burial. From the three gifts is also derived the belief that the Magi were three, even though antiquity provides us with conflicting numbers.

Even this homage of the pagans was certainly joyous, a happy surprise for the little family which for a day interrupted its usual anonymity. But even on this occasion, to their joy at the recognition given to the baby, for the gifts, for the festive welcome, sorrow was not long in coming. The finale was decisively tragic. The Magi were advised in a dream not to return to Herod; Joseph was advised, also in a dream, to flee at once into Egypt, that is abroad, "because Herod is going to search for the child in order to kill him."

History refers to Herod the Great as the genial builder of grandiose buildings, including the rebuilding of the Temple of Jerusalem. But it also speaks of his exceptional cruelty, especially against political rivals or pretenders to the throne. Among his many slaughters we recall that he massacred three of his own sons and two wives. Jealous of power, he managed to obtain from the Romans the title of king and could not tolerate the thought of any possible rivals. That is why he was so disturbed by the Magi's question: "Where is the newborn king of the Jews?" For such a cruel sovereign it was nothing to have all the baby boys two years old or younger from the village of Bethlehem killed. As regards the number, it is estimated that there could have been between twenty and thirty. He didn't hesitate to carry out this horrible crime as soon as he became aware that he had been tricked by the Magi who had returned to their own land without coming back to him to tell him where this baby, the future king, was. It was a horrible crime, as is every taking of a human life. But this does not remove the outrage over the horrible slaughter of innocents, who in the millions are killed in our so-called civilized nations, with the approval of aberrant laws.

Simeon's prophecy began very soon, all too soon, to be fulfilled: Jesus will be a sign that will be opposed and Mary's heart would be pierced by a sword. The shepherds and the Magi went in search of the child to adore him; Herod sought him in order to kill him. For some, the presence of Jesus, even though he came for our salvation, was immediately an inconvenience. We can imagine how the annunciation given by the angel of the imminent danger which threatened the child put wings to the feet of the Holy Family. They fled at once, thus sharing in the plight of refugees everywhere, the politically persecuted, those who are forced by human treachery to leave everyone and everything to face the unknown in a strange land.

We know that the evangelist Matthew wrote his story keeping above all the needs of the Jewish Christians in mind, and for this reason he likes to emphasize the fulfillment of prophecies. In telling us about the presence of Jesus in Bethlehem, he recalls three prophecies. The first is that the Messiah would be born in Bethlehem, in conformity with the indications foretold by Micah. Then, in recounting the massacre of the holy innocents, he recalls what Jeremiah wrote about the tears of Rachel: thus he commemorates the tears of all mothers whose sons are killed. Finally he recalls the prophecy of Hosea, "I have called my son from Egypt," to say that even the exile of Jesus and then his return had been prophesied. Especially in the last two cases we notice a certain liberty of interpretation and of adaptation: it is very significant in helping us understand just how rich Sacred Scripture is in meaning. It often presents figures or episodes which take on multiple meanings. Sometimes certain references which would elude us have light thrown on them by the Holy Spirit who is the principal author of the Bible.

In the episodes which we have considered, from the pious visit of the Magi to the cruel massacre of Herod, there is a succession of facts, behavior, states of soul, which merits a more intent consideration. The center of it all is the person of Jesus. It is he who stirs up reactions that are so diverse, according to which his presence is either welcomed or rejected.

Reflections

About Mary — We see in her a rapid alternating between joy and sorrow: joy when her son is recognized, loved, and adored; sorrow when he remains misunderstood or even assailed. It is right to think even of her sorrow over the massacre of the innocents: what fault did they have? Could it be possible that her son, the Son of God, might be the occasion for the unleashing of such treachery? Perhaps on this occasion, too, Mary's faith was put to a harsh test: the Son of God was forced to flee before a mean and deceitful man.

About us — This episode forces us to reflect on how we are often called to take a position: with the Magi or with Herod. To be Christians and to live as Christians can at times be very inconvenient and even stir up the ire of the others. How many persecutions down through history, past and contemporary, have there been! On our part there can be the temptation to line up with those who are strongest, to go along with the crowd, or to give in to our passions and personal interests. And our faith can be put into crisis by the comportment of God, who does not always intervene in conformity with our way of seeing things.

Home Coming

"Flee to Egypt and stay there until I tell you," the angel had said to Joseph. Heaven was certainly watching over that precious family. The flight had been precipitous, with fear of being followed and caught, until they had managed to cross the border. It is highly probable that the family followed the caravan route which led from Beersheba to the sea passing near Gaza; from there they would follow another caravan route down the Mediterranean coast to Alexandria. It was known as the *via maris* (the sea road), which Joseph had come to know about from the tales of various merchants and beduins: a trip of about 400 kilometers or 250 miles, which would have taken some twenty days on foot.

Where would they have set up housekeeping? Tradition, albeit late (4th century and later), is unanimous in situating the residence of the Holy Family in the outskirts of Cairo, probably near a settlement of Jewish families who were not hard to find in Egypt. A few kilometers from Cairo, in a place called Matarieh, a centuries old sycamore known as "the Virgin's tree" is surrounded by an enclosure. But we know nothing for certain, except the fact that their stay in Egypt was protracted until they were given new instructions. They surely would have arranged things as best they could with that uncertainty typical of exiles, persons passing through, who live supported by the hope of being able to return soon to their own homeland. It is reasonable to presume that Joseph took up his trade, starting all over from scratch. He would have had to apply himself diligently in order to win the esteem and trust of a whole new clientele.

One is inclined to think that their exile did not last long. At the time of the massacre of the innocents, Herod was nearing the end of his life. Finally, an angel came again, always in a dream to instruct Joseph: "Get up, take the child and its mother and leave for the land of Israel — those who sought the child's life are dead" (Mt 2:20). At last, the hoped for announcement: you can go home again. Not only is Herod dead, but all those who sought the life of the child were gone. Perhaps the angel wanted to reassure Joseph as forcefully as he could that there was absolutely no one left who would attempt to kill Jesus; or perhaps he wanted to repeat the words which God addressed to Moses when he was fleeing from Egypt to save himself from Pharaoh: "…all those who sought your life are dead" (Ex 4:19).

And so once again the little family was on the move, retracing more or less the itinerary of their flight, but with an entirely different state of mind. There was no longer any danger and they were not facing into the unknown, heading into a strange land. Rather they were returning to their own country, to their own people, relatives and friends. Along the way, before reaching Bethlehem where Joseph had thought to return, he came to know from some of his companions on the trip or from some venders that he met news regarding the situation which he would find there. Herod had left a will, ratified by the Romans, in which he left Palestine divided between his two sons. Judea and Samaria went under the domination of Archelaus; Galilee and Perea under Herod Antipas. This was a true mess because that meant that even Bethlehem, in Judea, was governed by Archelaus. He was one of the worst sons of Herod. From his father he inherited, not his greatness, but only his cruelty and dissolute lifestyle, so much so that eventually, in 6 AD, Augustus deported him and kept him in exile in Gaul on account of his vices and excesses.

Joseph had a moment of hesitation, and justly so, about returning to a place where such a perverse man ruled. Again an angel in a dream confirmed the validity of his fears, and so he decided to return to Nazareth, his birthplace. Having arrived there, we can imagine the festive welcome their relatives and friends gave them. We should mention here also a detail regarding the Jews: all property, house or land, no matter how poor, is kept with great respect for the legitimate owner, even if he should be absent for several years. We can imagine the joy of going back to their own home, modest as it may have been. The little Jesus, who may have been three or four years old, showed up in Nazareth for the first time and would certainly have been at the center of their happy welcome.

At this point, Matthew, so careful about not letting slip any possible verification of a prophecy, presents a true puzzle for poor biblical scholars. He says that the choice of Nazareth had been made also because thus "was fulfilled the saying of the prophets: 'He will be called a Nazorean'" (Mt 2:23). It is a vague reference about which we find absolutely no mention in the Old Testament. With more simplicity and clarity Mark and Luke speak of Jesus, the "Nazorean," that is an inhabitant of Nazareth. We know that the first Christians were called "Nazarenes," that is, followers of one from the obscure village of Nazareth, a term usually uttered with a certain tone of disdain. Only in the cosmopolitan city of Antioch, where the first mass conversion of pagans took place, was the name "Christian" first used to indicate the followers of Christ, a name which would remain definitive.

From the usage and the customs of the time, we can get some idea of the daily life of the little family. Jesus, when he was about five, would begin to regularly frequent the synagogue and to learn a trade from his father. Mary took care of the house and garden. Each day she would go to the fountain to get water, reliving the days of her childhood. The whole day was lived in an atmosphere of prayer. For the Jews there is no distinction between holy and profane times; every action is rendered sacred by the benediction which accompanies it, a little like our prayers before meals. We know of a hundred of these blessings which offer God every action. The modest, humble life of the Son of God and his holy parents, in appearance insignificant, teaches us the great value of actions performed in an ordinary fashion, but done with love and offered to God. Holiness does not lie in accomplishing extraordinary works, but in living the life of everyday in a holy way.

Reflections

About Mary — Her faith-filled stay in a foreign land: that is what the Father wants, so I want it too. The joy of returning to her homeland , the joy that her son might be able to grow up and be educated in a Jewish environment. Her complete trust in Joseph and the satisfaction of knowing that he was enlightened by God. The humble unfolding of her daily life which hid from everyone the true greatness of God's Son and hers. The arduous life back then: caring for the house and garden (certainly Mary's hands were calloused from working in the their little plot), providing for the domestic animals, grinding grain to make bread, etc.

About us — To know how to wait for the unfolding of God's plans with full availability and trust. The ways of God are often those which cost the most sacrifice. The burden of daily work, to earn our bread with the sweat of our brow; the monotony of daily life; to perform every action with love, offering it to God: this is the normal way in which we sanctify ourselves.

A Troubled Mother

We usually refer to this episode as "the finding of the child Jesus in the Temple." In reality the event leads us to a consideration of the mission of Jesus as Teacher, of his awareness of being the Son of God, and of the redemption by means of the cross. It is an event of great prophetic importance, the only one that the Gospels report, almost interrupting the long silence regarding the years passed by Jesus in Nazareth.

A serious study, which we will limit ourselves to mentioning here, tells us of the real importance of the episode. Jerusalem, for St. Luke, as we have already said, is the city of the crucifixion. His evangelical account is developed as the unique itinerary of Jesus toward Jerusalem where he will undergo his passion. The other two times in which Luke speaks of the presence of Jesus in the Holy City also have a direct reference to Calvary. We have already seen how Jesus was presented in the Temple: the prophecy of Simeon over the little baby and his mother contain a very precise reference. Also in this episode of the twelve-year-old youth, even though it does not appear at first glance, the reference to the paschal mystery is implicit and confers on the event a significance of prediction and of preparation.

Let us take a look at its more profound value. The loss of Jesus, his disappearance, is an indication of what his death will be like. The

61

three days of searching anxiously to see him again point to the three days he spent in the sepulcher. The happy finding of him again is a foreshadowing of his glorious resurrection. We can see then, dimly, the drama of the cross with its aspect of atrocious suffering orientated to a joyous conclusion. Thus the event is seen as a prophetic anticipation and preparation for the paschal mystery, the mystery of death and resurrection, of sorrow transformed into joy, of defeat changed into victory.

Let us pause over some details. The scribes and the Pharisees, in the areas adjacent to the Temple, show themselves very welcoming towards the young men who had come up to Jerusalem on the occasion of the Passover. It was for these young men a precious occasion to approach those great experts of Sacred Scripture on whose study and preaching they dedicated their lives. Often there were famous personages, whose judgments were referred to even in the most widely scattered villages. In the family it was the father who would read and explain the Bible; then there was always some instruction in the synagogue in which all the men present could intervene. But in Jerusalem were to be found those whom we would call the most famous theologians or university teachers.

The intelligence of Jesus and his responses are the object of wonder. It's hard not to think what his teaching will one day be, "given with authority." It is most probable that the doctors and those present were struck in seeing how this youngster from Nazareth, that is, from a city of no importance whatever and deprived of a rabbinical school, could have so much zeal and such knowledge of the word of God, and how he could know how to respond so wisely to the questions which were asked of him. It is unthinkable that he would have demonstrated any kind of originality; more likely he would have incited admiration on account of his love for the word of God and for his zeal in interpreting it in a way that conformed more to its spirit than to its letter.

The fact that he remained in the city without his parents being aware of it is easily explained if one thinks how travel in caravans took place: everyone left in stages toward the first fixed stop; the youngsters could go with whomever they wanted. Only when the stop was reached did the families get together again, and when the last group arrived they realized who was missing. Thus after the first day of the journey from Jerusalem and the second with another caravan going back to the city, finally on the third day the parents found their son, where they certainly must have thought he might be.

There is no doubt that the importance is heightened by the question of Mary, still center stage, and the mysterious reply of Jesus. "Son, why have you done this?" Perhaps, given the knowledge that the mother had of her son, the question might have included several explanations: "Did you have some particular decision in sight on the eve of your becoming an adult, at 13? Are you already putting your program into execution? Have we failed you in some way? Is your life about to take a new turn?" The sorrow suffered by them in those days lovingly bursts from her lips: "Your father and I have been searching for you with great anxiety." With great anxiety: Luke uses the same words to indicate the pain of hell. And for these holy parents these truly have been three days of hell.

And now we hear the very first words of Jesus reported in the Gospels: "But why were you looking for me?" It's not easy to understand a question that answers another question. Perhaps he is making reference to when his parents had offered him to the Father, with an oblation to which Mary was fully associated. Even more mysterious is the other interrogative: "Did you not know that I had to occupy myself with the things (or the house) of my Father?" Here there are three clear antitheses: the house of his Father and the house of his parents; obedience to his Father and obedience to his parents; the person of his true Father with respect to his Davidic father who is not humiliated but reminded of his own role.

It is an answer that remains obscure to Mary and Joseph, so much so that the Gospel affirms: "They did not understand." They knew the joy of finding him again, which is a prelude to the joy of Easter. But the observation of Isaiah almost spontaneously comes to mind: "You are a mysterious God" (Is 45:15). It is perhaps a veiled preparation for the many sufferings that Mary will undergo without at once understanding. Even for her there are some "why's" that have no answer here on this earth, as there will be for Jesus himself, when he will cry from the cross: "My God, my God, why have you abandoned me?" The answer will come only after, and Jesus himself will give it to the disciples on the road to Emmaus: "Was it not necessary that the Messiah suffer all these things in order to enter into his glory?" (Lk 24:26). The answer does not come from the cross and death, but from the resurrection. At the conclusion of the episode we see that the holy spouses ask no more questions; they trust in God and return home where Jesus behaves himself as a most obedient son.

Reflections

About Mary — The Lord did not spare her either the sorrow or the torment of not understanding. It is always painful for a mother not to understand her own child. Mary is the one who always trusted God with her eyes closed, without any pretense of needing an explanation. The occasion of this great suffering was the ritual visit to Jerusalem. Sometimes the Lord asks us to make the greatest sacrifices precisely in those moments in which it seems to us to be more meritorious. And still this test for Mary was a gift, a necessary preparation.

About us — We are mystified if life presents us with many "why's" to which we are unable to give an answer: the child who is born mongoloid; the couple who want to have children and have none; all the vast field of evil and suffering. We have to trust ourselves to God. The explanations will come later; they will be complete only in the next life. Making our will correspond to that of God is true wisdom, even if we do not comprehend the motives.

This whole episode confirms the absolute primacy of God, even when it comes to those persons who wield great authority and are most dear to us. Our duty toward God takes absolute priority over any other kind of duty.

A Precious Silence

After the episode of the stay in the Temple, when Jesus was twelve years old, the Gospels only speak of him again when he begins his public life. They are silent for nearly twenty years, namely, for the longest period of his earthly life. And still this period lived under the obedience of his parents and at work, this period of human and spiritual maturation, in which Jesus "grew in wisdom, age and grace before God and man" (Lk 2:52), has a lot to teach us if we but strive to penetrate that silence just a little. We have already mentioned how Mary kept and meditated in her heart all those things which had to do with her divine son. We also said that, in conformity with Hebrew custom, she would never have withdrawn from her obligation of giving witness when the occasion required it. Did she ever speak of these twenty years? It's certainly possible; but in this case it is the evangelists who have kept silent because, as we never tire of repeating, their scope was not historical-biographical, but to proclaim the message of salvation.

And still we seek to penetrate that silence, because even this period of his life was lived by Jesus for us and for our salvation. Jesus is always the great and only teacher: when he speaks, when he acts, and when he is silent. Perhaps it is precisely this daily monotony that has a lot to teach us, because it is so like the common unfolding of our days.

A contemporary writer, a Jew who is very open and respectful towards Catholics, does not hesitate to affirm that these were the most "Jewish" years of the life of Jesus, that is, the years in which he lived and was educated as a pious Jew in keeping with the law given by God to the Chosen People, without anything exceptional, following only the practices established in those places in that day and age. I am speaking of the writer Robert Aron who, making use of the profound knowledge that he has been acquiring regarding those times, has sought to deepen the research in this area. We are indebted to him for two interesting and very useful books: *Gli anni oscuri di Gesù* (Ed. Mondadori) and *Così pregava l'ebreo Gesù* (Ed. Marietti).

Paul himself insists on the Jewishness of Jesus and on the merits of the Chosen People. "But when the fullness of time had come, God sent forth his Son, born of a woman, born under the Law, to redeem those who were under the Law, so that we could be adopted as sons of God" (Gal 4:4-5). And also "...from them [the Israelites] came the Messiah according to the flesh — may God who is over all be blessed forever" (Rm 9:4-5). We can not gloss over the radical turnabout that the Second Vatican Council took in its way of looking at the Jewish world with an eye to recognizing how the coming of the Messiah was prepared for in the Chosen People; hence the most appropriate and beautiful gesture paid to them by Pope John Paul II on the occasion of his visit to the synagogue of Rome was to call the Jews "our elder brothers."

But the principal fact, about which I think the Son of God wanted to instruct us, is that holiness does not lie in great works, but in living uprightly day by day. They will have been serene years, but not idyllic. The village life of those days was hard and full of fatigue, sustained by constant prayer and reciprocal love. It certainly does not seem that Jesus' behavior stood out in people's eyes for any reason, especially if his fellow citizens marveled when he began his public life and they came to know of the miracles he was performing. Even this seems to be a sign that, in those years, he did nothing extraordinary. If occasionally he spoke up to explain Sacred Scripture in the synagogue, something easy to imagine in such a tiny village, he would have done it with a great deal of zeal, but without that authority that he would demonstrate in his public life. Could he have done any more or any better? Is it possible that the Son of God would waste his talents for such a long time in obscurity? Here, too, in this there is an important lesson: there is nothing more perfect than to do the will of God; and Jesus waited serenely for indications of that will from his heavenly Father.

But there is one episode that certainly must have taken place in these years even if the Gospels don't speak of it because of its private importance: the death of Joseph. During the public life of Jesus, Joseph no longer appears and Mary must have been living with her relatives, as was customary for women who were alone. Moreover, when the Synoptics refer to the wonder the Nazarenes manifested for all that Jesus had begun to do, Luke expresses himself with the words: "Is this not the son of Joseph?" whereas, strangely, Matthew and Mark say: "Is this not the son of Mary?" They seem to be indicating that by this time his neighbors were used to seeing Jesus only with his mother.

Between Mary and Joseph, with common purpose and common vicissitudes, there must have developed an ever growing love. I believe that one could say that never was a husband more loved than Joseph and never was a wife more loved than Mary. Perhaps only such a chaste love, combined with a sublime purpose, could reach such profound refinement and affinity. Mary will come to understand ever more the treasure she has in her husband, helpmate, and friend whom the Lord had assigned to her.

For Jesus, then, who called Joseph *Abba* (daddy) first, he was truly the image of the heavenly Father. Joseph gave him all the best that a father can give his son: a human education, a respected name, knowledge of God. He taught him how to pray, to work, and gave him the constant example of an upright life. That is why I find reductive certain names commonly attributed to Joseph such as putative father, foster father and the like. Joseph is the Davidic father of Jesus: he gave him, above all, membership in the house of David in fulfillment of the prophets.

We usually invoke St. Joseph as the patron of a happy death, because he certainly breathed his last in the solicitous care of Jesus and Mary; it's impossible to think of any better assistance. Did they pray to the Father to cure him? We can be certain that they did. But, as Jesus will do in the Garden of Olives, they would have subordinated their request to the will of God. This just man had finished his mission and was ready for Heaven. Jesus not only wept over his friend Lazarus and over the city of Jerusalem. He surely wept over Joseph, too. And Mary, besides her great sorrow, began a new mission, common to so many women: that of being a model widow.

Reflections

About Mary — More than ever we see how she was sanctified in her life as a housewife, a very hard life in those times for the poor. The common fatigue of each day makes us feel more than ever that she is our sister. Every day, filled with prayer and work, was a gift of God. She spent herself for the Son of God; but all mothers, all fathers, spend themselves for the children of God, from the moment that Jesus said that whatever we do for one another we do for him.

About us — The principal reflection has to do with our understanding of the value of ordinary life, hidden and monotonous, if it is offered to the Lord, if it is lived in grace. For this it is necessary that it be interwoven with prayer. Even the lives of those who are widowed, of those who are alone, of those who never realized their dream, perhaps, of a love and family, are precious if lived in grace. And, as the Bible says, the death of the just man is precious in the eyes of God.

The Wedding Feast at Cana

In order of time, the Gospel of John is the last. He doesn't repeat what is in the writings of the Synoptics, but tells us things that we don't find in the other Gospels. Regarding Mary, the apostle whom Jesus loved tells us exclusively of two interventions of Mary: at Cana and at the foot of the cross.

The framework of the salvific episode of Cana is a joyous nuptial feast. We find ourselves at the very beginning of the public life of Jesus, when, having left Nazareth, he had himself baptized by John in the Jordan, and then, during the forty days of fasting in the desert, he had come face to face with Satan, his adversary. Together with his first disciples, he takes part in the wedding feast at Cana, a village not far from Nazareth. Mary arrives before him. The evangelist highlights her presence almost as if to insinuate to us that where Mary is Jesus arrives; or perhaps it is she herself who had her son invited. He comes when the wedding feast is already underway, a wedding feast, as we have already indicated, that commonly lasted seven days.

The nuptial feast is only the framework around matters far more important. It is enough to realize that no description whatsoever of the couple, the protagonists of the feast, is given. The importance of this narrative lies somewhere else. Let us say at once that one of the purposes of the story, which is apparent at first sight is the *consequence* of this miracle of Jesus, justly called a "sign," namely, to manifest his divinity, even if it will be understood only a little at a time, in a way that will give rise to faith in him on the part of his first followers. In fact the story ends with the words: "And his disciples believed in him."

But there are also other meanings which the evangelist pauses over at some length. These come from the presence of Mary, from the initiative she takes, and from the brief dialogue that she has with Jesus and then with the servants. First of all, there is an occasion. The mother of Jesus (as John always calls her; he never uses her name), probably related to the spouses as was usual in similar occasions, ready to give a hand in the unfolding of the feast, notices a grave inconvenience which would have humiliated the spouses and interrupted the festivities. She asks nothing explicitly; God does not need our advice. She simply says to Jesus: "They have no more wine."

The response of her son, which some exegetes hold to be the most difficult phrase in John's Gospel to interpret, has to be understood in its context: "What do you want from me, woman? My hour has not yet come." The first words, also translated as "What is that to you and me?", we find at other times in Sacred Scripture to indicate a refusal. Here the meaning is clearly altogether different and only comes to light as the entire episode unfolds.

Also the term *woman*, while respectful, can seem a slight compared to that of *mother* which we were expecting. Instead it contains a very precise biblical reference, which scans the role of Mary in five fundamental moments in human history. (1) "I will place enmity between you and the *woman*" (Gn 3:15): This is the first proclamation regarding Mary which coincides with the first proclamation of salvation. (2) "When the fullness of time came, God sent his Son, born of a *woman*" (Gal 4:4): in these words Paul expresses the humanity of Christ. (3) Here at Cana, the word *woman* introduces a turning point, and we will see that right away as Jesus prepares himself to promulgate a new law. (4) From the cross, the same word, *woman*, will confer on Mary a new maternity. (5) At the end of the world, the *woman* clothed with the sun will appear as a great sign of salvation. Thus Jesus here confirms that Mary is the *woman* who has such a fundamental role in human history.

"My *hour* has not yet come." In the Gospel of John, the *hour* of Jesus always indicates the paschal mystery. Here perhaps he sets up an appointment, after a period of detachment, when the *hour* will have come and the two will meet again on Calvary. Jesus' reply is not and it is not to be understood as a refusal. In fact he goes on to perform the miracle. Rather it has a much more profound significance, according to which Mary, inserted as we have seen in the whole plan of redemption, here takes on the role of mediation which we must discover. In fact, she addresses that invitation to the servant: "Do whatever he tells you," which is not only the testament of Mary (the last words which the Bible attributes to her); they are not only those which, down through the centuries, will be repeated each time her voice is heard in extraordinary apparitions. Here the meaning is more profound yet.

Biblical scholars note that John, in this narrative, follows the grand scheme of the biblical covenants: the first is that of Sinai which then is renewed several times in the course of the history of Israel. Always, in these covenants, there is a mediator. On Sinai it is Moses, at Cana it is Mary. There is also always a phrase repeated that indicates acceptance of the word of God. On Sinai the people say: "Whatever the Lord tells us we will do"; at Cana it is the Madonna who says: "Do whatever he tells you." On Sinai God responds to this availability by giving the norms of the Old Covenant, the Decalogue; at Cana Jesus responds to the availability of the servants by giving new wine. The old wine which has run out represents the Old Covenant; the new wine, which is better and is placed at their disposition in abundance, indicates the New Covenant, the new doctrine of the Gospel, which Jesus sets out to preach and in which the disciples, encouraged by that first *sign*, have already come to believe.

We now see clearly the value of the joyous framework offered by the nuptial feast. Often wedding feasts are recalled by the Gospel as a sign of the heavenly reign, of the eternal nuptials with the Lamb; that is they signify the eternal felicity of Paradise. Here again is the general overall meaning of the episode. In the festive framework of the wedding feast, Jesus initiates the New Covenant giving new wine, i.e., his doctrine. It is good to underscore the role of Mary, and the importance of this first miracle in solidifying the faith of the disciples.

Reflections

About Mary — "Through Mary to Jesus" (*Per mariam ad Jesum*). Whenever one goes to Mary he or she finds Jesus. Her power of intercession never goes against the plans of God, but is always a catalyst for its realization. She doesn't ask the servants to obey her, but Jesus. These, her last words, "Do whatever he tells you," sum up well her desires, her suggestions, that which she recommends to each one of us.

About us — It is not necessary to see miracles in order to believe; the word of God is enough. Let us renew our faith in the person of Jesus, true God and true man, as the apostles knew and believed in him. Let us renew our pact with the Divine Master: our baptismal vows, our adherence to all the teachings of his Gospel. And let us place our trust in the powerful intercession of Mary, to whom Jesus always responds. Let us think of the goodness of Jesus as he addresses our human needs. What a beautiful thing it is that he would have performed his first miracle to bring joy to a nuptial feast! May his presence never be lacking between couples and in their families.

In the Obscurity of Nazareth

"After this he, as well as his mother and brothers and his disciples, went down to Capharnaum and stayed there for a few days" (Jn 1:12). These are the only days in which we hear that Mary has the joy of staying with her son during his public life. Thus she sees the little center on Lake Gennesaret, chosen by Jesus as the point of departure for his preaching in Galilee. Then Mary returns to Nazareth, where she remains for the rest of her son's public life.

In those times social security did not exist, but there was no room for solitude. We have only to think of the many times the Bible encourages and eulogizes those who care for orphans and widows. When a widow was alone, she went to live with her relatives. And I imagine that Mary must have done so for all the rest of her life. Among the relatives of Jesus, numerous as is the case in all Eastern families, there was room for every possible attitude toward the mission undertaken by the Son of God: he had relatives who were his followers in Jerusalem, who will remain faithful until after his death, and it is easy to think that the Virgin went to live with them; he had relatives who were his adversaries, those who took him for crazy and tried to interrupt his ministry; and he had relatives, probably a large number of them, who were indifferent.

In order to better understand the position of Jesus during his public life, we have to refer to Jewish customs. Work was held in high esteem, as a necessary and obligatory means of sustenance. Jesus himself, for as long as he lived privately in Nazareth, maintained himself by working as a carpenter. But when a person dedicated himself to being a rabbi, that is, to preaching the Sacred Scripture full time, he ceased to work with his hands and lived on alms, he and his disciples; thus he could move about freely from one place to another. To give an example closer to our own time, we think of the lifestyle of the mendicant orders up to the last World War. There was always someone whose job it was to go begging: that which could be used in the monastery was consumed, the rest was distributed to the poor. Jesus and his apostles lived in this manner: they lived on alms and gave what was left over to the poor.

Even on this point St. Paul broke with Judaism. Preaching in a pagan atmosphere, where such a practice was unknown and would not have been appreciated, he renounced this Jewish right and continued to practice his own trade. More than once he repeated, not without a certain pride, that he provided for his own needs and those of his collaborators by the work of his own hands.

But let us get back to the life of Mary in Nazareth. How different it must have been from when she lived in her own home, with the persons she most loved and who most loved her! Some may wonder why the Madonna, staying alone, did not join the women followers of Jesus. The reason is evident. The small apostolic group had no need, as we might think, of someone to wash dishes and prepare their meals. All Jews, when it comes to their own personal needs, know how to provide for themselves. They only needed financial or material aid. The Gospel clearly affirms, in enumerating the women who followed Jesus and the apostles, that they "provided for them out of their resources" (Lk 8:3). Even Mary Magdalene, who has nothing to do with the unnamed sinner of the Gospel nor with Mary of Bethany, must have been well-to-do. The Virgin Mary instead was poor; she wasn't in a position to contribute to their expenses; and so she could not follow her son.

Certainly she would have heard the echo of his discourses, of his miracles, and even of his diatribes with the scribes and Pharisees. There will have been those who rejoiced with her for having such a son, and those who would have criticized her for the same reason. It is most probable that she would have continued to frequent the Temple on the occasion of Passover (John speaks of three Passovers that Jesus spent in Jerusalem during his public life, and from this information we deduce that the public life of Jesus lasted three years); then she would have directly heard her son. She had likewise heard him on that unfortunate visit to Nazareth which provoked in Jesus that sad indictment: "No prophet is accepted in his own native place" (Lk 4:24). Not only that, but his beloved neighbors wanted to kill him by hurling him down from the brow of the hill on which their town was built. Even today at Nazareth there is a little church called St. Mary's Tremors to recall Mary's anxiety on that occasion.

The Synoptics report an exception which seems due more to the will of his relatives than to an initiative on the part of Mary. "One day his mother and brothers showed up where he was, but they couldn't get near him because of the crowds. So he was informed, 'Your mother and your brothers are standing outside and wish to see you.' But in answer he said to them, 'My mother and brothers are those who hear the word of God and put it into practice'" (Lk 8:19-21).

It is a brief response that has a twofold value. In the first place, Jesus announces a new kind of relationship with him, not based on natural bonds, but on hearing his word. In the second place, it indicates to us the true greatness of Mary: even before her maternity, she was great because she heard and practiced his word; she is the most faithful disciple. Vatican II specifically cited this text (LG 58) to exalt the Blessed Virgin.

Were there other encounters between Jesus and Mary not reported in the Gospels? It is probable, but in this case the evangelists have considered them episodes of private value only. Certainly the heart of Mary, her thoughts, her preoccupations were constantly directed toward her son and his activities. We imagine that the Lord wanted to present us with a great lesson in this period of the life of Mary: namely, how we can efficaciously collaborate in the apostolate even in the obscurity of an ordinary life, offered with love to God, in the acceptance of his will each day and offering for that purpose the prayers, fatigue, and suffering that life presents. It is for this reason, coming down to our own times, that we see associated as patrons of the missions St. Francis Xavier, the great preacher of the Orient, and St. Thérèse of Lisieux, who never set foot outside her convent.

Reflections

About Mary — Certainly it cost her immeasurably to have been set aside. After having spent her life and her activity directly on the person of her son, she is seen to be set apart. But she accepted with total generosity this, the Father's will. She understood that her hidden life was not useless, as she awaited that great appointment which came to her in Cana when the hour of Jesus would come. With prayer and a life lived in conformity with the teachings of her son, the model for all his followers, she is in her own right an example for us.

About us — A true and intimate relationship with Jesus is acquired by listening to and putting his words into practice; what counts is a life in conformity with the teachings of Christ. The wish to follow him is not enough: "Not everyone who says to me 'Lord, Lord,' will enter the kingdom of heaven, but only the one who does the will of my Father" (Mt 7:21). When waiting in obscurity costs more than direct action, let us think that what always counts most is to do the will of God.

Woman, Behold Your Son

"Now standing by the cross of Jesus were his *mother* and his *mother's* sister, Mary the wife of Cleopas, and Mary Magdalene. When Jesus saw his *mother* and the disciple whom he loved standing beside her, he said to his *mother*, 'Woman, here is your son!' Then he said to the disciple, 'Here is your *mother*.' And from that hour the disciple took her into his home" (Jn 19:25-27).

It is the *hour* of Jesus, the *hour* for which he became incarnate. And Mary returns to the fore: for her it is a second annunciation, one in which she is proclaimed mother of all humankind. As usual, John does not call her by name, but rather by her role. That role is well indicated by a word which we have emphasized because it is repeated five times in just three verses: *mother*. From that hour the mother of Jesus is proclaimed our mother too: "Woman, here is your son." For Jesus this is the fulfillment of his messianic work on earth; death will follow at once. For Mary it is the beginning of a new maternity. How she would have preferred to die with her son! But her mission was not finished and is not finished yet. Jesus is not at all worried about making sure that Mary is taken care of: she is already with relatives and will remain with them. We are the ones who have need of a mother.

"Here is your mother." At this point the disciple whom Jesus loved makes a gesture of great significance, a gesture which indicates comprehension and acceptance of this new relationship created by Christ. This time Mary's consent was not required; she was already wholly vowed to Jesus and his work; her consent had already been pronounced fully and definitively, without conditions or limits, with the *fiat* she spoke to the angel Gabriel. At this point it was the *believer* in Christ, the beloved disciple, who had to express acceptance. "And from that hour the disciple took her into his home." We would like to add: among his many goods as believer, because John represents the disciples who have believed in Jesus and have received the goods necessary for salvation: faith, the Eucharist, the Holy Spirit, Mary. John understands that Mary is one of the goods necessary to salvation, and he accepts her as such. "Can one be Christian if he is not Marian?", Pope Paul VI will ask in Bonaria on April 24, 1970. God has willed to give us Jesus by means of Mary. We can never subtract ourselves from this selection made by the Father. If we do not understand the role of Mary towards Jesus, we will never understand Mary's role towards each one of us. We will insist again on this acceptance, which lies at the base of our consecration to Mary and of the maternity of Mary with respect to the Church.

But at this point it will be rewarding if we pause for a few moments over an argument which to our way of thinking has great importance and which is generally overlooked: Mary's feelings at that moment. Her immense sorrow is evident. The liturgy applies to the Virgin the passage of Lamentations (1:12): "Come, all you who pass by the way; look and see whether there is any suffering like my suffering," almost as if to say to us that there has never been a sorrow such as hers. The poets have given us the *Stabat Mater*, the various "lamentations" of Mary over her dead son, the "Pianto" of Jacopone da Todi; painters and sculptors have reproduced the "Pietà" and the "Addolorata," before whom people pray with great fervor. All this is very true; but there are other feelings about which it is important to reflect, because they give us the measure of Mary's heroic faith.

Above all in Mary's soul there is no room for any kind of rancor, rebellion, resentment or the like. She saw around her only persons whom Jesus had just given to her as her children. Vatican Council II tells us that in that moment she associated herself in her mother's heart to the sacrifice of Jesus, "lovingly consenting to the immolation of this victim which was born of her" (LG 58). *Consenting*: This is the newest and the strongest word of this great Marian document. She was certainly not consenting to the evil, to the killing, to the blasphemies, to the verbal challenges. She was consenting to the will of God, to that will which Jesus had fully accepted. A tremendous will can cause the heart to bleed more than martyrdom itself. And still she accepts it with total adhesion: such has the Father willed, such has Jesus willed, to this will Mary also gave her suffering adhesion.

There is another aspect, no less important, that helps us understand the source, the light which brought Mary such heroic strength, such a total adhesion of faith at the death of her son. She understood, and in that moment only she, the *value* of what was taking place, the value of that death. Perhaps the Virgin Mary, in the whole arc of her life, especially during the public activity of Jesus, may have felt continually echoing within her the uplifting and prophetic words of Gabriel: "He will be great, and God will give him the throne of David, his father. He will rule forever over the house of Jacob and his kingdom will have no end." Fleeting words which allow one to glimpse a glorious future, a success without precedent.

So here we see the heroic faith of Mary challenge the clearest possible evidence before her eyes. While she sees Jesus in agony and death, Mary understands that the prophetic words of Gabriel are being fulfilled. Certainly, they are being fulfilled in the most unthinkable and most atrocious possible way, but they are being realized. For the others, that death is a failure. It is the end of a dream, of a great hope, as the disconsolate two disciples on the road to Emmaus will later say. For Mary it is not that because she understands that it is in precisely that way, contrary to every human expectation and much more of every maternal expectation, that the triumph of Christ is taking place, his victory over sin and death, the redemption of humanity.

Another thought immediately comes to mind: Mary understands that it is from that death that the world is saved and that she herself is redeemed. And it is in the strength of that terrible death that she is all that she is: immaculate, always a virgin, the mother of God.... It is in the strength of that death that all generations will call her blessed because the Almighty has done great things in her. But Mary is never so great as she is in that moment of her sorrowful *fiat*; never had she had to demonstrate to such an extent a faith so profound. It is thus that Christ reigns and saves. Her heart bleeds, but she says, "Thank you." She thanks God for herself and she thanks him for all of us: she is saved, we are saved. The culminating sentiment of Mary at the foot of the cross is one of profound gratitude.

Reflections

About Mary — Jesus pardons from the cross; Mary relives that pardon toward each one of us, even if we sin. She teaches us to see the hand of God even in sorrow and in our broken hopes. She teaches us what true faith is, to believe even against that which seems so evident. She teaches us to thank Jesus for his sacrifice.

About us — Let us make a profound examination of the value of the sacrifice of Christ, of its redemptive power, of our gratitude and correspondence, so that it may never be lost on us. Have we accepted Mary as our true mother in the plan of salvation? Have we learned to believe, to hope, to pardon with all our heart, to thank God even in our suffering?

The obedience of Christ redeems the disobedience of Adam; Mary's participation redeems the participation of Eve. But our obedience to God is necessary if we are to receive the fruits of the redemption.

The Sabbath, Mary's Day

It almost seems that, in the great Paschal Triduum, there is a void, a silent and pregnant pause, between the crucifixion and the resurrection. But this void is filled by a person whose heart is full of hope and certitude, because her faith, and only her faith, has not crumbled. God had foretold in Genesis that she would be the sign that the Savior would come; her birth is saluted as the breaking dawn that foretells the sun, Christ. Holy Saturday is the day usually given to Mary, and the practice of celebrating "Mary's Hour" on that day is becoming ever more widespread. In all the world hope is alive only in her, because only she awaits faithfully the hour of triumph.

The others, no. For the others that Sabbath is yet another day of anguish, rich only in sorrowful memories, the unknown, darkness. The thoughts of the main witnesses could not dwell on anything other than that sad recollection: the atrocious death of Jesus, with its humiliating contours, made still more shameful by the conduct of his friends. The betrayal of Judas, who had put an end to his life as an apostle with that desperation that brought him to hang himself, had been consummated; Satan had truly entered into him. Peter, so impulsive and generous, after his triple denial, had no other alternative than to shed bitter tears of regret. The other apostles knew no better way out than to flee; they were not yet able to throw off their fear of being hunted, and so they stayed behind closed doors.

Even the women, the most faithful to Jesus, mingled with their tears a sole practical preoccupation: that of finishing the embalming of the dead body of Christ, since on that Friday evening his burial had taken place so hastily because the "Great Sabbath" was about to begin.

The loss of all hope and the impression that "everything was finished" is evident in all of them. They never would have thought that "everything was about to begin." None of them thought that the blood poured out for the New Covenant signaled the way for the new People of God. The resurrection will come as one of those surprises that one finds difficult to believe, for which proofs will follow one after the other. First the empty tomb and the angels who proclaim: "He is not here. He has risen." Then the various apparitions to individuals, groups, a crowd of about five hundred faithful. The paschal liturgy will be characterized by the joyous song addressed to the Virgin: "Rejoice, O Queen of heaven, rejoice; the son whom you merited to bear has risen as he said. Alleluia."

But meanwhile, on that silent Sabbath, the torch of humanity's faith is wholly and only burning brightly in Mary. For her it would have been a great liberation to be able to die with her son; but she had to initiate her new mission as our mother, which she received from her agonizing son. Even to this she had given her *fiat*; and her mission began right then on that Sabbath, offering to God something very precious, of which no one took notice: an unflagging faith. She alone believes and thinks what no one else thinks or believes; she alone is prepared for the great event, which no one else expected. She may perhaps have reflected on that third day in which she found Jesus in the Temple; or to another third day when her son arrived in Cana and changed the water into wine; or to Holy Thursday when he had changed the wine into his blood. Perhaps she thought back to the words, undoubtedly referring to his resurrection, that Jesus, foretelling his passion always ended with, a phrase which the apostles never understood: "And on the third day he will rise." It is certain that her heart was full of hope and certitude.

And yet that Sabbath unfolded strangely. The guards took turns watching over the sealed tomb, with the cadaver inside, as if man could put limits on the omnipotence of God. All the people throughout the city were feasting because they were celebrating the Passover; they were not aware that their Passover was a prophetic sign of a great reality that had begun in sorrow and was about to be fulfilled in joy. A tomb under strict surveillance, the celebration of a rite which has no more sense, are two of the many anachronisms of that day in which the only valid thing is the faith of Mary, her certainty about that which was about to happen and which will definitively turn around the prospects of human life.

Thus Saturday will become Mary's day, the day of preparation for the Sunday of the resurrection which will supplant the Hebrew Sabbath as the feast day for all Christians. There will be a gradual cultural and liturgical deepening, arriving in the ninth century at an official dedication of Saturday to Mary with the Mass and Office proper to the Virgin. But the first step, the point of departure, lies precisely in the importance that the Madonna had on that Holy Saturday.

The dawn of Sunday finally broke. We see a small group of women, very early in the morning, arriving at the sepulcher. They are the same ones whom we saw at the foot of the cross. But one is missing, the most important. How in the world is it that Mary is not with them? It is a meaningful absence. Perhaps the risen Lord has already appeared to her, even if the Gospels do not say so. Or perhaps she is so certain of his resurrection that she did not make the mistake that the other women made, to seek the living among the dead. We can think what we like, but we can be sure that she didn't go to the tomb because there was a strong reason which held her back.

The women, admirable for their fidelity and their zeal will find a surprise: the tomb is empty. Because of this even the mute stones take on a special importance. By the fact of the tomb's being empty they become the first witnesses to the resurrection of Christ. And it is for this reason, too, that the Holy Sepulcher will become the dearest, most loved and most visited of Christian shrines.

Afterwards various apparitions of the Risen One will follow, for which the disciples of Jesus will pass on from one to the other the joyous news: "Jesus Christ lives!" Even today, after 2000 years, the responsibility of Christians is to shout to all: "Jesus Christ lives!" It is this happy news that saves.

Reflections

About Mary — Her faith is heroic, but there is no doubt that it had a strong foundation which nurtured it, and it is the same basis on which our faith is also nurtured: incessant prayer and a profound meditation on the words and works of her son. Without these helps even her faith would not have been sustained. When the Bible speaks to us about the faith of Abraham, it tells us that he believed against all hope, that is against all the evidence the facts presented. Pope John Paul II used to say that Mary's faith is greater than that of Abraham. Abraham did not see his son die; Mary did. But she believed all the same.

About us — The promises of God never become less, as his love and his aid do not become less. When things go well it can seem very easy to have faith; but faith is tried in the midst of contradictions. The observation that the greatest sorrows, the greatest sufferings put our faith to the test is true for everyone: either it becomes stronger or we lose it. Even we need to have recourse to the double aid, of prayer and meditation on the word of God.

Fire from Heaven

Pentecost furnishes St. Luke an occasion to highlight once again the presence of Mary at the birth of the Church. The sacred text lists the eleven apostles who have come together and adds: "They all devoted themselves single-mindedly to prayer, along with some women and the mother of Jesus and his brothers" (Ac 1:14). We see at once the prominence given to the presence of Mary who, besides the other apostles, is the only person mentioned by name, with the detail of her glorious qualification as mother of the Lord.

Not many days earlier an important event had taken place, to which certainly the persons just mentioned took part, even if this is not said so expressly: the ascension of Jesus into heaven. It is an important and joyous episode. Along with the resurrection, the glorification of the human body of Christ and the entrance of his human nature into his glory (as Jesus himself tells it in speaking to his disciples on the road to Emmaus) is emphasized. With the ascension the humanity of Christ also acquires that power of intercession that he uses at once to send the Spirit and continues to use always in our favor. Before ascending into heaven, Jesus gives his last instructions to his own: "Do not leave Jerusalem until you have been baptized by the Holy Spirit." From the Holy Spirit they would receive the strength to be his witnesses in Jerusalem and in all Judea and Samaria, even to the ends of the earth.

We can imagine the joy that Mary herself experienced assisting at the ascension of her son to the Father, the prelude of that moment when she, too, would be taken up in a definitive way, with no more separation. In the meantime, in obedience to her son, she prays, invoking the descent of the Holy Spirit. Her presence is precious, expressly affirmed, because it is the beginning of that presence and assistance that Mary will never cease to have in favor of the Church and each one of its children. It is pleasant to think of her in this way as she is described in this final mention which the New Testament makes of her: present and in an attitude of prayer. For this reason we never tire of invoking her help: "Pray for us, sinners...." The Second Vatican Council emphasizes the role of Mary at Pentecost, to implore "the gift of the Spirit [on the apostles], who had already overshadowed her in the Annunciation" (LG 59).

The Spirit, descending under the form of tongues of fire, immediately manifests a reference to the Word: that divine Word which the Spirit has the mission to recall and to explain, and that the apostles have the duty of preaching. The first success is had with the sermon of St. Peter: three thousand at one time and five thousand at another ask to be baptized.... Perhaps only then did Peter understand the significance of Jesus' words: "From now on you will be fishers of men," him, a fisherman who was overwhelmed when in a single net he had captured 153 fish. Now it is the Church that initiates its journey with an initial explosion that recalls the prophecy of Isaiah: "Can a country be brought forth in one day, or a nation be born in a single instant? Rejoice with Jerusalem and be glad" (Is 66:8). Mary is a member and the mother of this new people.

We are brought to reflect, too, on what fruits this new effusion of the Holy Spirit might have brought to Mary. It is easy to suppose that, besides an increase in union with God and of peace, the Virgin might have had still greater light for understanding the words and the life of her son. These same episodes that had caused her to marvel or which she did not understand, will have become ever clearer to her. It is true, the Spirit had already descended on her several times with specific effects: to suggest to her a life of total virginity; to overshadow her and cause her son to be conceived; to watch over and sustain her in the various stages of her life; above all to illuminate her at the foot of the cross. It is easy to think that the new effusion of the Holy Spirit at Pentecost, other than to enlighten her ever more on the life of her son, would have given her a profusion of the graces necessary for the fulfillment of her new mission as our mother and mother of the Church.

It is useful to reflect on this detail: the Holy Spirit can be received many times, indeed without limit, with a growing increase of fruits. He descend on us in baptism; with even greater strength at our Confirmation; and then all the times that we invoke him, because the Lord has said: "The Father will give the Holy Spirit to those who ask him for it" (Lk 11:13). For that reason we must never tire of invoking him, in order to always and with more clarity listen to and follow his voice, so different from that of the flesh and of the world, and in order to arrive at that full imitation of Christ which the Lord expects from us.

The life of the Virgin ends in obscurity. It is the moment of the apostles, of the evangelists, the deacons. Successes alternate with persecutions, but the good news continues to spread. Mary most holy will have followed it all, encouraging and participating. There are also the first martyrs: the deacon Stephen and then the apostle James, the brother of John. Mary's presence will have been a comfort to all, while her testimony enlightened the sacred writers about what she alone could know, above all about the birth and infancy of Jesus.

Where did she spend her last years? I believe that she never moved from Jerusalem. The tradition that prefers Ephesus, with the apostle John, is very late and is explained in a variety of ways, in its origin and from recently discovered documents. A bishop from Ephesus in the ninth century, Eutimius, decried the fact that the scourge of brigands had made it almost impossible for pilgrims to go to Jerusalem to pray at the sepulcher of the Dormition of Mary and to celebrate the Feast of the Assumption. This would explain why he then had constructed at Ephesus the little church of the Dormition. If this unfolding of events can ever be historically proved, it would indicate that the memorial church at Ephesus was built not on account of the presence of Mary in that city, but for reasons of cult. In any case, when the Lord willed, the Virgin was taken by "sister death," to which she gave her ultimate *fiat*.

Reflections

About Mary — Let us consider her joy of contemplating, with faith, the presence of Jesus at the right hand of the Father after the ascension, and her awaiting his return. Her prayer together with that of the apostles that she continues with the Church and alongside each one of us. The effect on her of the descent of the Holy Spirit. The comfort that he gives in times of persecution; all these sufferings foretold by the Lord. Her serene return to the Father's house.

About us — Let us entrust ourselves fully in prayer made in the name of Jesus, because he intercedes incessantly for us. Let us continually invoke the Holy Spirit, especially in moments of greater need for light, in order to live in conformity with the will of God and to grow in our conformation to Christ. Let us entrust ourselves to the presence of Mary at our side, having received the role of being our mother. Let us think serenely of death that enables us to reach the definitive goal of our existence.

Wholly Glorified

What was Mary's participation in the resurrection of Christ? We always want to have everything at once. In the eyes of God, time has an altogether different value. We think that the real participation of Mary in the paschal event was her assumption. St. Paul reminds us that it will happen to each one of us, at the resurrection of the flesh, obtained thanks to the resurrection of Christ, when our bodies too will rise incorruptible and immortal. All this, for Mary, took place immediately after her death. What happened on November 1, 1950, when Pope Pius XII solemnly proclaimed the dogma of the Assumption in St. Peter's Square, is still vivid in the memories of many. It was truly *the* culminating day of that Holy Year. It had to do with an event whose truth is contained in the Bible, but only implicitly. A long period of study was required before it would emerge in all its clarity.

The procedure followed by the pope, which repeated that which Pope Pius IX had followed in arriving at his proclamation of the dogma of the Immaculate Conception, is interesting. Long before, in 1940, Pope Pius XII had instituted a commission to interrogate the people of God, through all the bishops of the world, to find out what the faithful believed and what they desired. Keep in mind a principle that Vatican II expressed in these words: "The whole body of the faithful... cannot err in matters of belief when 'from the bishops to the last of the faithful' they manifest a universal consent in matters of faith and morals" (LG 12). It is a case of real and true infallibility.

The outcome was substantially unanimous. Thus Pius XII "confirmed the faith of the brethren," as Jesus recommended to St. Peter, affirming: "The Immaculate Mother of God, Mary ever Virgin, when the course of her earthly life was ended, was taken up body and soul into the glory of heaven" (*Munificentissimus Deus*). As we can see, the assumption of Mary is declared a dogma of the faith. Pius XII did not want to weigh the text down with any pronouncement about whether Mary had died or not. It was a question debated in the past, taking into account that in Mary there was no original sin, which subjected all of humanity to death. Today scholars are in agreement that, as Jesus submitted himself to death, so Mary also died. Pope John Paul II has affirmed this as a personal conviction of his. But we believe that today the question is moot.

What interests us most is to observe how dogmatic definitions are often provoked by disputes and errors which require a precise response, or by a desire to solemnly affirm a truth believed for centuries and celebrated in the liturgy, even though not explicitly contained in Sacred Scripture. Thus the first thing that is done is to define the terms, setting forth the difficulties. Even after the dogmatic definition, the foundations and the consequences continue to be studied.

In the past we used to like above all to extol the greatness of a person, putting emphasis on their privileges; today we prefer to emphasize the services they rendered on the plane of salvation. These two aspects are not contradictory but need to be integrated, each one being true. For this reason in the past we stressed, in the Assumption, the fulfillment of the redemption since Mary was glorified in body and soul. In theology, it was expressed by the term: wholly redeemed. Mary's conformity with her son was highlighted: it was only right and just that she be associated to his glorification having been associated with him in the whole work of the redemption, especially in the paschal mystery. Insistence was placed on the appropriateness of the fact that that flesh from which Jesus had received his own flesh should be glorified, and it was added: as, through the merits of Christ, exemption from original sin was applied to her preventively, so it is only right that preventively the fruits of the redemption likewise be applied to her.

All of these are valid arguments, held even today. But today we prefer to add other motives. Every privilege is given to Mary in view of a scope that exceeds the personal sphere; even her assumption does not escape this criteria. For that reason it was not conceded to Mary only to honor her person, but in view of a salvific event. Mary had received from Jesus a new mission which will last till the end of the world: her maternity over all humankind in the economy of salvation. Her mission on earth is not finished, as it is finished for other human beings who can only contribute with their prayers in the communion of saints. For Mary this is not the case. It was therefore necessary that she be found in the totality of her person, body and soul, in order to carry out this new mission in our favor.

Now the body of Mary, like that of Jesus, is no longer tied to time and space. Therefore, their presence alongside each one of us is unceasing. To offer an example, think back to the various apparitions of the risen Lord. He gave the impression of entering and exiting a room even though the doors were closed. This has given rise on the part of theologians to efforts in understanding the properties of a risen body, among them subtlety. The reality is something different. Jesus told us clearly that he would remain with us always, even to the end of time, and so he is always present. When he wants to appear, he makes this presence visible; then, once he has achieved his purpose, he again renders himself imperceivable to our human senses. Still his presence continues.

The same thing happens with Mary. And even more, not only has her presence no limits in space and time, as they did when she lived on earth in only one place and for a limited amount of time like all of us; then even her activity could be limited by hours which pass and don't return. Now this is no longer so. Her maternal care over us has no limits and, as the Second Vatican Council says, it is a work that will continue until all men are led into their blessed home (cf. LG 62).

In this way it is easy to understand the reasons and the consequences of the assumption of Mary. Assumed into heaven, she is alive and, as our true mother, is always at our side with a presence that is ever active even if we do not see it. Hers is a constant and total presence because it is no longer bound by the limits of space and time that she herself had during her earthly life. It is a maternal and efficacious presence in the order of salvation which we describe by the titles with which we address her: Mediatrix of All Graces, Refuge of Sinners, Advocate, Help of Christians.

Reflections

About Mary — Let us contemplate her, fully redeemed, in the felicity of the whole of her human person, body and soul, to which the saints themselves aspire and to which we all tend; the true first fruits of humanity glorified, on account of the merits and in total dependence on Christ glorified. Notice the gifts which God has given her, even that of having assumed her into heaven body and soul for our advantage. Then let us think of her solicitude toward each one of us.

About us — Let us realize that Mary is always at our side and let us feel her near, even if we do not see her. On account of this, let us have continual and trustful recourse to her. We will know only in heaven how much we have cost her and what she has done for us, the dangers from which she has saved us, the inspirations that she has given us, the strength which she has infused in us, the graces she has obtained for us; and all this without our even being aware of it. Whoever reflects seriously on these truths, on the constant presence of Jesus and Mary at our side, will live full of confidence and will never suffer from a feeling of solitude.

There Appeared in the Heavens a Great Sign

Only God is eternal. For that reason before anything existed there was only God in the dynamism of that love which is innate to the three persons united in one divine nature. Then creation, the angels, the cosmos and mankind, saw this love express itself externally, giving life to creatures who were only beautiful and good, creatures in whom the Creator took great pleasure. But the most beautiful gift, which constitutes the grandeur of the superior creatures, intelligence and freedom, induced first one part of the angels and then, through their instigation, our first parents to pride and rebellion. Thus sin entered the world along with evil, suffering, death and hell when God had created it all for eternal happiness.

Satan's hatred for God brought him and brings him to seduce human beings to rebellion and sin. But against the consequences of original sin, the infinite mercy of God foretells salvation. He will send his own Son, who will be our redeemer. He will be the son of a woman. This woman, immediately announced, is placed by God himself as the enemy of Satan. It is the first annunciation regarding Mary at the dawn of human life. Here is the text of the protogospel, or first annunciation of the redemption: "I will place enmity between you and the woman [It is God himself who is creating this irreconcilable rivalry], between your seed and her seed; this one [that is, the son of that woman] will strike at your head and you will strike at his heel" (Gn 3:15).

Mary is already foretold as a sign of salvation and as an enemy of Satan. It is a text whose true significance will become better understood over time. We have used a translation which faithfully reproduces the Hebrew text. The Greek translation, called the Septuagint, uses a masculine pronoun which is a precise reference to the Messiah: "*He* will strike at your head." The Latin translation of St. Jerome, known as the Vulgate, though, translated it with a feminine pronoun: "*She* will strike at your head," favoring an interpretation that is wholly Marian, an interpretation that was preferred by most of the ancient Fathers of the Church, from Irenaeus on. It is clear that the one who conquers Satan is Jesus. The action of Mary is always and only dependent on that of her son. With precision the Second Vatican Council correctly states: "[The Virgin Mary] devoted herself totally, as a handmaid of the Lord, to the person and work of her son, under and with him, serving the mystery of redemption" (LG 56). For this reason all the images which show Mary in the act of crushing the head of the serpent, so long as this gesture is seen as cooperation in the work of her son come to destroy the works of Satan, are legitimate.

At the end of human history we see a repetition of the same scene. The woman reappears as a sign of salvation and reappears in the posture of one in combat against Satan. Here is the text: "A great sign appeared in the sky, a woman clothed with the sun, with the moon under her feet and on her head a crown of twelve stars.... Then another sign appeared in the sky; it was a huge red dragon, with seven heads and ten horns... the ancient serpent who is called the Devil and Satan, who deceived the whole world" (Rv 12:1ff.). Who is that woman? Often in the Bible the same figure can represent a multiplicity of subjects. The woman can represent the Church; she can represent the Jewish people; she surely represents Mary, since Jesus is her son.

So Mary is the sign of salvation, from the beginning to the end of humanity. St. Bernard liked to say and to write: "Mary is the whole reason for my hope." An aside: this was the phrase written on the door of Padre Pio's cell. Who knows how many times the holy friar repeated it? But at this point we are invited to reflect on what Mary's role will be at the end of the world. We know well the fundamental part that she had at the first coming of Christ. But then, when Christ ascended into heaven, and the apostles with Mary continued to stand there looking up in his direction, two angels came to interrupt their trance and declare: "This Jesus who has been taken from you up to heaven will return in the same way you saw him going up to heaven" (Ac 1:11). The Lord will come again; the Lord will return: *Marana tha!* Come, Lord Jesus. The eschatological tension, the awaiting of the Parousia (the glorious return of Christ), is typical of times of living faith, even though we do not know the date. Thus the Gospel invites us to always be ready, as we must always be ready for the arrival of "sister death."

But what will Mary's role be on that occasion? The saints, particularly St. Louis Grignon de Montfort, hold that the Virgin Mary will have a very important and evident role. Her freely given "yes," by will of God, preceded the incarnation of the Word. Mary, at the first coming of Christ was mother and collaborator of the Redeemer, but in a very discrete way . For the second coming of the Lord, which will be a glorious return, the role of Mary will instead be apparent to all: it will be she who will prepare "the apostles of the end times," as Montfort used to like to put it, and to conduct the fight against the red dragon. That is the reason for the sign that appears in the heavens, the woman clothed with the sun.

Meanwhile the enmity will continue and the battle will be without respite. Paul is very clear: "Put on God's armor so you'll be able to stand up against the schemes of the Devil, for we're not engaged in a struggle with mere flesh and blood — we're fighting against the rulers and powers, against the cosmic powers of this dark world, against the spiritual forces of evil in the heavens" (Eph 6:11-13).

Mary is the victor, thanks to her son, and she helps us in the fight. What is her secret? One day, an exorcist from Brescia, the late Father Faustino Negrini, asked the Devil: "Why are you so afraid when I call upon the Virgin Mary?" And he heard him reply with a stupendous apologia: "Because she is the most humble of all creatures and I am the most proud; she is the most obedient and I am the most rebellious; she is the purest and I, the most defiled." Another exorcist, aware of this response, several years later asked Satan: "You exalted Mary because she is the most humble, obedient and pure of all creatures. What is the fourth virtue that makes you tremble?" and he immediately received the response: "She is the only creature who can conquer me entirely, because she has never been defiled by the slightest shadow of sin."

The battle for each one is strong; what is at stake is eternal salvation. But there is no cause for fear. We have the grace merited by Jesus and we have the help of the Blessed Virgin Mary.

Reflections

About Mary — The role of Mary, there is no doubt, has continued to be ever more fully understood and discovered down through the history of the Church. And at the same time her cult, both liturgical and popular, has progressively increased. Her strength against Satan, owing to that fourth virtue which we mentioned, is a model for us too. We don't know the plans God has for Mary in preparing the Parousia; but we do know the help that she gives us now, as our mother in the order of salvation, and hence, in particular, in the order of our battle against sin.

About us — Let us reexamine our commitment to continual conversion and purification, our preparation. The Gospel tells us to be vigilant, always ready for the coming of the Lord: death can overtake us at any moment. Let us have recourse to Mary's aid, to her invocations, to her prayers, especially in our fight against temptation. And let us trust in the power of Mary to intercede for us.

Mother of the Church

After a lengthy re-elaboration, preceded by harsh dissent, the Second Vatican Council approved, on November 21, 1964, the Constitution on the Church, *Lumen gentium*, containing an eighth chapter dedicated entirely to the Virgin Mary. The crowning of that chapter took place when Pope Paul VI promulgated, in front of the whole Council, the title it had attributed to Mary, *Mother of the Church*, with the purpose of acknowledging a truth amply contained in the Marian document they had approved which, in part, compensated for other titles desired by a large part of the conciliar Fathers, of which it was preferred not to make an official declaration. The first of all these titles would have been "Universal Mediatrix of Grace."

Here are the words of the Holy Father: "We declare the most holy Mary 'Mother of the Church,' that is, of the entire Christian people, faithful and pastors alike, who call her their most loving mother.... Divine Motherhood is the reason why Mary is related to Christ in a unique way and is present in the work performed by Jesus Christ for the salvation of humankind. Similarly, her divine motherhood is also the main source of the relationship between Mary and the Church. Indeed, Mary is the Mother of Christ who, while assuming human nature in her virginal womb, united to himself as Head his Mystical Body which is the Church. Hence, as Mother of Christ she must also be considered mother of all the faithful and pastors, that is, 'Mother of the Church'."

It is a title of great import. Even if the solemn proclamation was only made in 1964, we find it already understood in the maternity of Mary towards all of us, as illustrated by such Church Fathers as Irenaeus, Epiphanius, Ambrose, Augustine and others. Vatican Council II had hesitated before this title which proclaims Mary not only the mother of all individuals, but also of the ecclesial community as a whole. And still it had already included in this Marian document the expression used by Pope Benedict XIV in 1748: "The Catholic Church, taught by the Holy Spirit, honors Mary with filial devotion and affection as a most beloved mother" (LG 53).

The reasons behind the hesitation were two. Above all the Council wanted to make it clear that Mary is also a *member* of the Church, and her presence at Pentecost and her later participation in the Jerusalem community show her in this light. But it is also true that Mary is likewise a type and model of the Church itself: both virgins and mothers, generating children of God through the working of the Holy Spirit. Pope Paul VI will say: "One cannot speak of the Church if Mary is not present there" (*Marialis cultus* 28).

A second fear they had was this: that the title 'Mother of the Church' lends itself to misunderstanding, as if the Church had been born of Mary and not of Christ. Even this fear is a reasonable one, but it is enough to explain things. We have seen how the title 'Mother of God' could lend itself to even greater misunderstanding without adequate explanation. The title 'Mother of the Church' emphasizes the cooperation of Mary at the birth of the Church and in all its undertakings. It is a cooperation subordinate to and dependent on the action of Christ; but it is an evident cooperation, from the incarnation to Pentecost, from Pentecost to the Parousia. For this reason the Council took pains to underscore the role that Mary had and continues to have by virtue of the will of the Lord.

The Church was willed by Christ, not by men. It is the new People of God since "God willed to make men holy and save them, not as individuals without any bond or link between them, but rather to make them into a people who might acknowledge him and serve him in holiness" (LG 9). Even if immediately before this it is affirmed that "at all times and in every race anyone who fears God and does what is right has been acceptable to him," an affirmation all that more important because it is true that the royal road to salvation is indicated by the Lord in these words: "Whoever believes and is baptized will be saved; whoever does not believe will be condemned" (Mk 16:16). But it is just as true that God wills the salvation of all, that Jesus died for all for whom God reserves even other means to salvation which we do not know.

It is necessary to insist on the fact that the Church was founded by Christ, that he wanted it to prolong his mission, that he loves it and guides it with his grace and has given it the Holy Spirit as its very soul; that Mary is its mother and as such assists it. These are all important truths which should be carefully kept in mind because today, in general, the Church is not loved. From Christians themselves it is seen as something external to them ("the Church are the priests" is the current mentality), and the most pernicious errors today turn on the false conceptions that are had of the Church.

Certainly, the Church reflects, in an analogous way, the mystery of Christ, for which we can justifiably speak of "the mystery of the Church." The mystery of Christ is to be God and man: his contemporaries saw a man like any other who needed to eat, to sleep to relax. And yet these human characteristics, limited and weak, concealed the reality of his divine person in which his human nature and his divine nature were united. It was a mystery difficult to understand and at the same time tremendous. As a result, every time Jesus acted as God (forgiving sins or affirming: "Before Abraham came to be, I am"), he was immediately treated as a blasphemer. Even in the Church a mystery is concealed: it is made up of men, weak and sinners like the rest; and still it has been given divine powers: to preach the word of God with the efficacy of the Holy Spirit, to pardon or withhold the pardon of sins, to consecrate the Eucharist. It is the mystery of the Church: holy and human.

A particular aspect which would merit still greater study, is that the maternity of Mary over the Church does not only have to do with Catholics or Christians, but all people since the Church was instituted for the salvation of all. This is the way the Latin-American bishops put it in their Puebla Document (1979): "Mary has a heart as big as all the world and she implores the Lord of history for the sake of all people." Jesus had said to Peter: "Feed my lambs, feed my sheep" (Jn 21:15-17), that is, all humanity. I believe that the irresistible attraction that Pope John Paul II exercises over all peoples is a sign of this universality. In his trips, as in Thailand where Christians are very few, the crowds are unbelievable. It could not be solely because they are curious to see the representative of Catholics. We believe that, through an impulse of the Holy Spirit, the whole population feels a personal relationship with that white father come from Rome.

St. Cyprian affirmed: "One cannot have God for Father who does not have the Church for mother." Mary, Mother of the Church, helps us to understand and to love this truth.

Reflections

About Mary — Mary's presence at the ascension, at Pentecost, in the life of the Church is significant. Her presence in these two thousand years of the life of the Church is more significant yet. The People of God is very sensitive to this presence, as witness her cult, her sanctuaries, her continual invocation. Mary brings us to Jesus. Jesus has given us the Church. If we do not know how to follow this grace-filled itinerary, we render vain the care of the Virgin for the People of God.

About us — Let us try to comprehend the mystery of Christ, God and man; to comprehend the mystery of the Church in its human and divine aspects. The title of Mary, Mother of the Church, tells us of her love and care for this work of her son. Following the example of Mary, it is necessary that we learn how to love the Church if we want to be pleasing to the Lord and to participate in the fruits of the redemption.

The Immaculate Heart of Mary

In the Bible the heart expresses the entire make-up of the interior life of a person. Thus God is often seen addressing the heart in order to act in depth on the whole person. And when, with the prophet Ezekiel, God promises to give a new heart, it indicates a total conversion to him on the part of his people who had completely gone astray. For this reason to speak of the heart of Mary means to penetrate into the whole of her inner life, into her rapport with God and men. The phrase repeated by Luke, that Mary kept these events in her heart and meditated on them, makes direct mention of the heart of Mary. But it is only an initial beginning of a singular development which gradually grew down through the centuries and which has exploded especially in our time.

The patristic reflection on the heart of Mary insisted, especially with Augustine, in seeing in it "the treasure house of all mysteries," in particular of the mystery of the incarnation, arriving at the affirmation that "Mary had conceived in her heart before she conceived in her womb." Devotion to the heart of Mary developed ever more in the Middle Ages until, with St. John Eudes (who died in 1680), it acquired a rigorous theological explanation and officially received its own liturgical cult. The most recent developments took their impulse from here and can be defined by three occurrences. In 1830, the Virgin Mary appeared to St. Catherine Labouré, asking her to coin a medal, the famous "miraculous medal," which spread throughout the world in millions of copies, reproducing on the back the two hearts of Jesus and Mary, linking them together in the popular devotion of the faithful.

A second event which is significant for its repercussions in the Marian field took place when, after two centuries, in 1899 to be precise, Leo XIII consecrated the world to the Sacred Heart of Jesus. It was thought way back then that the time had matured to proceed also to the consecration of the world to the heart of Mary since the Lord had willed to associate Mary in all the works of salvation. Nothing came of it at the time though an impulse towards devotion to the heart of Mary and to the study of such a devotion did take place nonetheless.

There is no doubt that the apparitions of the Madonna at Fatima in 1917 gave rise to its greatest development. One might say that, as apparitions to St. Margaret Mary Alacoque provided a great impulse to devotion to the Sacred Heart of Jesus, so apparitions to the three shepherd children of Fatima provided a decisive impulse to devotion to the heart of Mary. Already for some time a new invocation had been introduced. In the past one only spoke of the "most pure heart," or "most holy heart" of Mary and similar expressions. After 1854, that is after the proclamation of the dogma of the Immaculate Conception, the expression "immaculate heart of Mary," which refers to the "heart of the Immaculate Mary," began to be used. In the apparition of June 13, 1917 at Fatima, the Madonna said: "God wants to establish in the world devotion to my immaculate heart." She then asked that Russia be consecrated to her immaculate heart. To Alexandrina Maria Da Costa she asked that the world be consecrated to it. From that time on one cannot count the sanctuaries, parishes, religious communities and associations which have come into existence with this title.

What is the value of this devotion, directed above all to invoke the intercession of Mary on us? In the first place, we must remember what the Second Vatican Council had to say: "Mary's function as mother of men in no way obscures or diminishes the unique mediation of Christ, but rather shows its power. But the Blessed

Virgin's salutary influence on men originates not from any inner necessity but from the disposition of God. It flows forth from the superabundance of the merits of Christ, rests on his mediation, depends entirely on it and draws all its power from it. It does not hinder in any way the immediate union of the faithful with Christ but on the contrary fosters it" (LG 60).

All this is very important for understanding what Mary means to us for our life as believers. It is God who freely willed to make use of Mary for his incarnation. He wanted to submit himself to her in his mortal life. He wanted to associate Mary to himself in the work of salvation and wills to continue the redemption of every person through Mary, to transmit to every believer divine life. He willed to unite Mary to himself in heavenly glory, making her a participant in his reign. It does not surprise us then, as the Madonna herself has said, that the Lord wills that the heart of Mary be honored along with the heart of Jesus. It is not a matter of sentimentalism, but of a profound commitment that involves the whole of one's being. The opposite of this devotion is formalism, that formalism which drew from the lips of Jesus the lament: "This people honors me with their lips but their hearts are far from me" (Mt 15:8).

In the history of the schools of spirituality, devotion to the heart of Mary is shown to be an inexhaustible fount for the interior life. Such was the case with the spirituality of Helfta, of the Benedictines, the Franciscans, and the Dominicans. It is interesting to notice how later St. Francis de Sales saw, in the heart of the Virgin, the meeting place of souls with the Holy Spirit. And it is important to point this fact out to those who fear that the devotees of Mary attribute to her the specific role of the Holy Spirit.

On the one hand, the heart of Mary encompasses the entire mystery of Mary, seen as a mystery of grace, of love, of total correspondence and total gift that Mary made of herself to God and to humanity. On the other hand, we cannot pass over in silence those Marian events that were the occasion for the development of such devotion. It is enough to think of Fatima. Other than a call to conversion and prayer; other than a reminder of the great truths such as our last ends; a particular emphasis was given to the Eucharist (one thinks of the reception of Holy Communion on the first Saturdays of each month in reparation for sins) and to the impulse for a generous reparation. It is sufficient to cite, in this regard, the encouragement expressed by the words: "Pray, pray a great deal for sinners, for many souls go to hell because there is no one to sacrifice and pray for them" (Fatima, August 19, 1917).

In Pius XII we seem to hear an echo of these words: "This is a tremendous mystery and one that is never adequately meditated on: namely that the salvation of many depends on the prayers and voluntary mortifications undertaken for this purpose by the members of the Mystical Body of Jesus Christ, and by the cooperation of pastors and faithful, especially by the mothers and fathers of families, in collaboration with the divine Savior" (*Mystici Corporis*, 42). Collaboration with the Savior! This *tremendous mystery* shows us how devotion to the immaculate heart of Mary underscores a love that saves and invites us to participate in the same salvific love, collaborating with Jesus in the eternal salvation of our brothers and sisters.

Reflections

About Mary — The heart of Mary highlights the total love of all her being for Jesus and for his brothers and sisters, in other words, for all her children. The heart of a mother invites and convinces with strength and tenderness. To honor the heart of the Immaculate Virgin Mary is to honor a heart that is totally pure: from sin and from every human conditioning. It thus spurs us to greater fidelity and imitation.

About us — Contemplating the heart of Mary, there is not only an attraction that spurs us on to fidelity; there must also be a disposition to imitate her, to open ourselves to God with all our heart, to follow the maternal admonitions of Mary. And how could we not recall the suffering heart of Mary, the heart of Mary pierced on account of our sins?

Marian Apparitions

Apparitions in general, and especially Marian apparitions which have been so frequent in these last centuries, cause us to take stock of their value and of what position we ought to take regarding them. Logically here we intend to speak only of those apparitions of a certain seriousness, not those of that swarm of pseudo-seers, pseudo-charismatics and the like, of whom the earth is full today who say and write rivers of messages, often catastrophic (already a sure indication of their falsity) who don't merit our consideration. But there do exist authentic apparitions, in whose regard a position (which has nothing to do with the virtue of prudence) that has already prejudged and discredited them is to be condemned since they may well turn out to be authentic interventions willed by God.

Not only the history of the Church, but the whole of sacred history is punctuated by apparitions. It is necessary then to keep in mind an essential distinction between biblical and extra-biblical apparitions. The apparitions reported by the Bible, for example to Abraham, to Moses, to the prophets, to St. Joseph (even in a dream God can send his messengers), to St. Peter, to St. Paul, etc., all these apparitions make up an integral part of divine revelation and have the same inspirational value as the rest of Sacred Scripture.

Extra-biblical apparitions, even if officially approved by ecclesiastical authority, remain private apparitions which add nothing to the patrimony of the faith, and their importance is highly diversified: for an individual, for a city, for a temporary situation. But they can also have great importance from the pastoral point of view. We immediately think of the importance of Guadalupe, of Lourdes, of Fatima. But it is good to repeat, with regard to all these private revelations, the concept that they add nothing to public revelation. Vatican II affirms this reality decisively: "No new public revelation is to be expected before the glorious manifestation of our Lord Jesus Christ" (DV 4). There is no room for any so-called "intermediate coming of Jesus Christ" which certain self-styled modern seers talk so much about.

For example. The crucifix that spoke to St. Francis had a very personal importance and many apparitions to the saints gave rise to their vocations and missions. The apparition of the Virgin Mary to Vincenza Pasini in 1476 was of great importance to the city of Vicenza which was being devastated by the plague. It even inspired the building of the Sanctuary of Monte Berico which to this day is the most visited in all of Veneto. The apparition of Our Lady of La Salette in 1846 was important for a whole region. She reminded the inhabitants of their duty to sanctify the feast days, to observe the Friday fast, not to blaspheme. And later on the sanctuary acquired an importance that transcended national borders.

But there have been Marian apparitions of an even great pastoral importance, such as to mark an epoch and continue for centuries. If we were to indicate which ones, in our opinion, have been the most important Marian apparitions in the history of the Church up to now, we would not hesitate to mention that of Guadalupe in the City of Mexico. Christianity risked being introduced into the Americas as one of many odious impositions of the new conquerors from across the sea, whose comportment left a great deal to be desired. The Virgin, appearing as one of the young women of the locality, an Aztec girl, opened the Christian faith to that population, especially in Latin America, also as a religion revealed directly to them.

Then we remember the apparitions at Lourdes in 1858 four years after the definition of the dogma of the Immaculate Conception. In this case the value has been very great. First of all the extraordinary fact of the apparitions and the miracles which followed had the importance of being a response from heaven to the ruling rationalism of the time. It was God himself who confounded the wisdom of the intelligentsia with the foolishness of a young girl who was almost illiterate yet chosen to be the ambassador of the Virgin. The pastoral importance is still evident today. One might even ask to what the faith in France might have been reduced had it not been for Lourdes.

Finally there is Fatima, which is *the* great Marian apparition willed by God to illuminate our dark century, made even darker by atheism and war. It is true, the religious aspect predominates: the recall to prayer, to conversion, to the three great truths of paradise, hell and purgatory. These all give to these apparitions the value of great pastoral importance which, moreover, have repercussions on public life. The Virgin said on July 13, 1917: "The war is about to end [the First World War]. But if they do not cease to offend God, under the pontificate of Pius XI another even worse war will begin." It is clear that the Madonna did not come to predict misery; she came to teach us how to avoid it; and that the Second World War was avoidable. One notes also that it is not God who castigates. It is men who, having moved away from God, castigate one another.

The great message continues: "If they listen to my requests Russia will be converted and there will be peace. If not, it will spread its errors throughout the world, causing wars and the persecution of the Church.... In the end my Immaculate Heart will triumph, the Holy Father will consecrate Russia to me that it might be converted [one cannot help thinking of all that has happened in Eastern Europe after that consecration on March 25, 1984]. And the world will be granted some time of peace." It is a message of exceptional importance which foretold all the future of the century which has just come to an end. "Wars are caused by the sins of men," the little Jacinta repeated at the suggestion of her great Mamma.

What value do these apparitions have? It seems clear to me: they are directly connected to the plan of salvation given for humanity and they are directly related to human life: social, political and economic. It is useless to create imaginary barriers, to relegate faith to the sacristy. In a world in which sex, violence, and horror (just open the pages of any newspaper or listen to the TV news) seem to dominate, the Madonna, like Jesus, who in his agony in the Garden of Gethsemane said: "Watch and pray that you may not fall into temptation" (Mt 26:41), sadly calls her children back to prayer and conversion. Thus the Marian message at Fatima ends with the grief-filled words: "May they never offend God, our Lord, again, who has already been so greatly offended."

Reflections

About Mary — There is no doubt that Mary's apparitions on all levels, whether they be of personal value or of value to the whole of humankind, make up part of her mission as our mother which Jesus entrusted to her from the cross. It would be an error not to put them always in relationship with the revealed word of which they are the faithful echo and application to actuality. But it would be no less wrong to undervalue their importance and, often, their urgency.

About us — The demeanor of those who run from one apparition to the other in search of the latest message is surely wrong. This is useless curiosity. We must listen to the words of the Virgin as a reminder of her testament: "Do whatever he tells you." In it we are strongly reminded of the words of Christ who has told us: "If you do not repent, you will all perish" (Lk 13:5).

I Consecrate Myself to You

Consecration to Mary boasts a very ancient history, even if it continues to be ongoing in its development during these last centuries. It comes spontaneously, as a point of departure, to have recourse to certain biblical texts. There are many of them, but I have chosen two. St. Paul: "I beg you by God's mercy to offer your whole lives as a living sacrifice which will be holy and pleasing to God" (Rm 12:1). St. Peter: "You are a chosen race, a royal priesthood, a holy nation, a people set apart by God to proclaim his saving deeds" (1 P 2:9). A people that shares in the royal, prophetic and sacerdotal functions of Christ is, of its nature, a consecrated people. Why then consecrate yourself to Mary, that is to God through Mary? The reason is: In order to understand and to live our baptismal consecration.

Pope John Paul II, on March 25, 1984, renewed the consecration of the world to the Immaculate Heart of Mary in union with all the bishops of the world who on the day before, in their own dioceses, had pronounced the same words of consecration. The formula chosen begins with the words of the most ancient of Marian prayers which goes back to the third century: "We fly to your protection...." It is interesting to note how such a prayer is already an act of entrustment to Mary on the part of the people. In fact collective consecrations are very ancient and precede individual consecrations.

Let us take an example. The formula of consecration of St.

Ildefonsus of Toledo (who died in 667) is very beautiful even though the first to use the expression "consecration to Mary" was St. John Damascene (who died in 749). Throughout the Middle Ages there was a race between cities and communes who "offered themselves" to Mary, often presenting her the keys of the city in a suggestive ceremony. But it is in the 17th century that the great national consecrations began: France in 1638, Portugal in 1644, Austria in 1647, Poland in 1656. Italy arrived late, in 1959, because it had not yet reached national unity and because the earlier proposals were never acted upon. After the apparitions at Fatima the consecrations multiplied ever more. We recall the consecration of the world pronounced by Pius XII in 1942, followed in 1952 by the consecration of the Russian people, again the work of the same pope. Many, many others followed and almost always, at the conclusion of a Marian pilgrimage, there was the consecration to the Immaculate Heart of Mary.

The consecration is a complex act and one which is a little different in each case. It is one thing when one of the faithful consecrates himself or herself personally, assuming specific obligations, and another when a whole people, nation or even humanity itself is consecrated. It is only right in these cases that the consecration be expressed in different ways as Pope Pius XII did from the very first consecration of the world for which he used three different verbs: I consecrate, I entrust, I remit. Not being able to say everything, we limit ourselves to some thoughts about individual consecration, theologically well explained by St. Louis Grignon de Montfort, and of which the pope is an ardent model with his motto *Totus tuus* (All yours), taken from Montfort himself, who in his turn had borrowed the expression from St. Bonaventure.

Let us give two reasons. The first is offered by the example of God the Father, who gave us Jesus through Mary, entrusting him to her. It follows that to consecrate ourselves to her is to recognize the divine maternity of the Virgin and is, following the example of this choice of the Father, the first reason that spurs us to consecrate ourselves to her. The second reason is the example of Jesus himself, Wisdom incarnate. He entrusted himself to Mary not only to draw his flesh and blood from her, but to be reared, educated and to grow under her watchful eye in wisdom, age and grace. Can we find a better person to be in charge of our formation than the person Jesus chose?

Let us add some of the consequences, namely, the commitments that we assume.

1. The commitment to imitate Mary who is not only the mother of the Lord, but also his most faithful disciple, the one who always said "yes" to the Lord, without putting any conditions. And, in order to be able to imitate her in her virtues so pleasing to God, we must get to know Mary ever more.

2. It is necessary to obey her, because she continually encourages us to obey Jesus. For this reason consecration to Mary is in God's plan for us to live as Christians. St. Louis Grignon de Montfort identifies this consecration as a renewal of our baptismal vows. It is therefore a renewal of our fidelity to God after the example and with the aid of the Blessed Virgin.

3. To consecrate ourselves to Mary is to take her into our life after the example of St. John. Mary has taken her maternal role over us very seriously. She treats us as her children, loves us as her children and provides us all we need as her children. It is up to us to recognize this spiritual maternity, to accept Mary into our life as believers, render her presence operative, favoring its action on us.

4. We cannot accept Mary if we do not accept our brothers and sisters who are also her children. We cannot accept Mary and feel ourselves to be her children without accepting the Church and feeling ourselves children of the Church. Certain expressions that you hear sometimes: "I believe in God, but I don't believe in priests," "I accept Christ, but not the Church," make no sense, above all in those who consecrate themselves to Mary, Mother of the Church. The new commandment is no longer sufficient, namely, that we love our neighbors as ourselves. It rather requires that we love each other "as I have loved you" (Jn 15:12). We don't love the mother if we don't love all her children.

5. A final thought cannot be overlooked: We consecrate ourselves to Mary also because we trust in her power of intercession. It is God who has made her so great, so powerful, for our advantage.

We know how very weak we are. Let us then recommend ourselves to Mary that she might pray for us "now and at the hour of our death," the two most important moments of our life.

We see now, from what we have said, that devotion to Mary does not consist, as unfortunately is the case for many, in having recourse to her only when we are in need. We don't love a person if we go to see them only when there is something we want to ask them for.

It seems to me that this brief panorama may be helpful. Let us begin, following the advice of St. Louis Grignon de Montfort, to live even only the first step of the consecration: to do everything *with Mary*. And we will see how in a few days it will totally change our lives.

Reflections

About Mary — All of Mary's titles and our whole relationship with her have their center in her maternal role: towards Jesus and towards us. She expressly asked that the world, Russia, and all people be consecrated to her because the Lord has willed it so: consecrated to her, she leads us to love Jesus and to keep his word. We see in this a great good for individuals and a great good for human society as a whole.

About us — We don't think that we are more intelligent than the Father who entrusted his only begotten Son to Mary. This is a clear example of the way to follow. Let us reflect on his reasons and on the duties implied in our consecration, to renew it and to live it more fully. Of its nature the consecration is not an act that is an end in itself, but a commitment that must be lived out day by day.

A Chain of Hail Mary's

As we begin to speak of the rosary, our thoughts go immediately to the definition which Pope Paul VI gave of it: "A compendium of all the Gospels." The fundamental characteristic of this prayer is to be at the same time a prayer and a meditation on the principal mysteries of our Christian faith. And for this reason, the Madonna at Fatima proposes the rosary as an antidote to atheism: the average person today has more need than ever to pray and meditate on the great revealed truths of the faith. The insistence of the popes in recommending this prayer (you think, for example, of the twelve encyclicals on the rosary penned by Leo XIII) does not surprise us, therefore, nor does the fact that insistence on this prayer played such a part in the apparitions of Lourdes and Fatima. John XXIII, with his endearing good cheer, let us, "his dear children," know that "the Pope's day is not over until I have recited the fifteen mysteries of the rosary."

The rosary did not come into being all at once. It is the fruit of a gradual evolution and we will understand it better if we review its long history over five centuries, from the twelfth to the seventeenth. We begin with the twelfth century, when the Hail Mary was widespread, limited, however, to just the first part. Prior to that time only the angel's salutation was recited (we have evidence of this from an antiphon of the sixth century, though not with the repetition we now know). For their part the monks recited the 150 psalms of the Bible, as they continue to do in the Liturgy of the Hours. For their lay confreres, who often did not even know how to read, 150 *Our Fathers* replaced the psalms and, to help them, they would use a circle of 150 beads for ease in keeping count. Notice that the use of a string of beads for counting prayers was already in vogue among Christians as well as among other religions even many centuries before Christ. When in the second half of the twelfth century, the *Hail Mary* replaced the *Our Father*, the Marian Psalter was born.

Only at the end of the fifteenth century did the use of the second part of the *Hail Mary* become widespread. Also at about that time the Cistercian Enrico di Kalkar had the happy idea of subdividing the 150 *Hail Mary's* into fifteen decades, separated by an *Our Father*. The more widespread the use of this prayer became, the more widespread were the confraternities of the rosary. A little later the meditations from episodes in the Gospels began to accompany the recitation of the rosary. Credit for having called the Psalter of the Virgin the "Rosary of the Blessed Virgin Mary," the name by which it is called to this day, goes to Alan de la Roche (who died in 1478). He also gets credit for the further subdivision into three parts of five decades each; and it was he who suggested the reflections on the mysteries of the incarnation, the passion and the glorification of Christ and of Mary. Finally, St. Pope Pius V, in 1569, wrote the first pontifical document which gave official sanction to the rosary.

This is how the synthesis in the rosary of prayer and meditation came about through an evolution over some five centuries. We are so subjected to distractions, especially when we pray. We risk in this way of reducing the rosary to a mechanical repetition of *Hail Mary's*, while the mind wanders on its own, absorbed by all kinds of thoughts other than those announced by the mystery. So it behooves us to resolve to make a serious effort to give back to the rosary the dignity and efficacy that is proper to it. When we recite it in common, we should follow a single rhythm, without rushing or dragging, as is done when we sing together. But when we recite it alone, a slower rhythm, one that is more contemplative, is recommended. It is true, the decades follow one another with a certain repetitiveness, and for that reason meditation on its mysteries is all the more necessary.

Bernadette was truly fortunate when, reciting the rosary in the grotto on the days of the apparitions, she saw the Madonna in front of her, who fingered the large beads of her rosary along with her. We ought to think, too, that the Madonna is always in front of us, even if we do not see her. The rosary is such a humble prayer that it can be adapted to all kinds of possibilities. It is best when we can recite it with tranquility, in church or at home. But it can also be used to fill our time on the bus, walking along the street, driving a car, waiting our turn at the supermarket. Reciting it alone, we pray for everyone. If we are in a group, the rosary itself, made up of beads held together by a single strand, invites us to union of soul.

The rhythm of modern life has broken the unity of the family. The members are rarely together and sometimes, even in those few moments, they hardly speak because they are given to reading or watching television. Pope Pius XII insisted on restoring the recitation of the rosary in the family. "If you recite the rosary together, you will enjoy peace in your families, you will have harmony of soul in your homes." "The family that prays together stays together," the American priest Father Patrick Peyton, the indefatigable apostle of the family rosary, used to say in every corner of the world. And Pope John Paul II reminds us: "Our heart can gather, in these decades of the rosary, the events which make up the life of the individual, of the family, of the nation, of the Church, of humanity. The rosary beats with the rhythm of our human life."

And it is also the prayer of peace, the prayer which embraces the whole world. Another great apostle of the rosary in our time, Archbishop Fulton J. Sheen, had the idea of a rosary in five colors, which is in use even today: a decade of green beads to recall Africa, famous for its green forests; a red decade for America, home of the native American Indians; a white decade for Europe in homage to the white vestments of the Pope; a blue decade for Oceania, set in the azure blue of the Pacific ocean; a yellow decade for the immense continent of Asia. In this way, at the end of the rosary we will have embraced the whole world.

The average person today has more need than ever to pause

for silence and reflection. In this hectic world prayerful silence is essential. If we think of the power of prayer, then we will be convinced that the rosary is more powerful than a nuclear bomb. True, it is a prayer that costs, that requires a certain amount of time. We, instead, are used to doing things quickly, especially when it comes to God. Perhaps the rosary will put us on our guard regarding that risk which Jesus warned Martha, the sister of Lazarus, about: "You are busy about many things, while one thing alone is necessary." We too run the same danger. We busy ourselves and preoccupy ourselves about so many contingencies that we forget that only one thing is necessary, and that is our rapport with God. The Founder of the Pauline Family, the Venerable Father James Alberione, liked to remind his sons and daughters: "We can all be replaced in every way but one: in saving our souls, in sanctifying ourselves. You must attend to this yourself, for no one else can take your place." It is time to open our eyes.

Reflections

About Mary — In the rosary, Pope Paul VI tells us, we meditate on the mysteries of Jesus in company with her who has most reflected on them and shared them. The gradual formation of this prayer has contributed to its richness. Let us slowly meditate from time to time on the *Hail Mary*, word for word, having recourse to Mary with the love of a child, trying to reconstruct the joy she must have felt on hearing the words of Gabriel and Elizabeth that spur her on to help us in making our own her supplication for the Church.

About us — Let us examine ourselves to see if we have understood the importance and richness of the rosary. With what sense of duty and frequency do we recite it? Perhaps now is the time to determine to make a concrete resolution. For Padre Pio, as for so many other saints, the rosary was the arms (that is what he called it) which he used to defeat the enemy.

Mediatrix of All Graces

In the ante-preparatory phase of the Second Vatican Council, which concluded in the spring of 1960, nearly five hundred Council Fathers including both bishops and prelates asked that the universal mediation of Mary be defined, but the proposal not to promulgate any new dogmas prevailed. As far back as 1921 Cardinal Mercier had presented a similar petition to the pope, immediately obtaining a specific Mass and Office for the dioceses of Belgium. The latest official appeal was presented by Cardinal Confalonieri, in the name of the chapter at Saint Mary Major's on March 2, 1984. Cardinal Ratzinger's response, that such a solemn pronouncement was not necessary, is interesting for its motivation: "The doctrine of the universal mediation of Mary most holy is already adequately found proposed in diverse documents of the Magisterium of the Church." In other words, it is already a certain and officially taught doctrine.

With this premise, we do not intend to defend a cause that has already been won, but to illustrate this Marian title, against all who hardheadedly side with the Protestants, erroneously anchoring themselves to the affirmation of St. Paul which no one contests: "There is but one mediator between God and men, the man Christ Jesus" (1 Tm 2:6). And still the whole history of the Church shows us how recourse to the intercession of Mary has been constant, in every circumstance of life. From the most ancient Marian prayer about which we have already spoken, "We fly to your protection," to the antiphons and invocations of the liturgy, to the popular witness of the votive offerings, today so highly valued once again, there is one harmonious voice.

The title of Mediatrix, given to Mary, goes back to at least the sixth century and was widely spread above all in the twelfth. The teaching of St. Bernard is well known: "We venerate Mary with all the impulses of our heart, of our affection, of our desires. Thus did He will who established that we receive all things through Mary." Dante gave poetic expression to these words in his famous lines: *"Donna, se' tanto grande a tanto vali / che qual [chiunque] vuol grazia ed a te non ricorre / sua disianza [desiderio] vuol volar senz'ali."* "Woman, you are so great and so powerful that whoever wants a favor or grace and does not have recourse to you, expects his desire to fly without wings."

There is no doubt that the sole mediator between man and God is Jesus and that "no one can go to the Father except through me" (Jn 14:6). But we have to understand the exact sense of these words so as not to make a fetish of them. Every time we use an adjective to describe God and to describe a human being, even if the words are identical, they are used with a different significance.

Let us give an example. The typical divine attribute, exclusive to God, is holiness: You alone are holy, only God is holy. This does not stop me from calling Peter, Paul, and Francis holy. But the word acquires another meaning. God is holy in an absolute sense. Paul is holy in a relative, limited, derivative sense dependent on the holiness of God in which, by divine gift, he becomes a participant. We can never say that Paul is holiness. With this difference understood, we will continue to say that only God is holy and that Paul is holy: the meaning is different, hence there is no contradiction.

The same application can be made with regard to the perfections of God and his mercy, inasmuch as the Lord admonished us to be holy as the Father, perfect as the Father, merciful as the Father. In reference to God we are talking about absolute attributes and their origin, and so we can say that God is perfection, that God is mercy. Referred to human beings, these same attributes have a limited, dependent value. They are a participation in the divine attributes conceded by the grace of God. The same concept holds also for the attribute "mediator." Referred to Jesus as its originator it has an absolute value. Referred to us it has a limited, subordinate, participatory value. Thus the word Mediatrix attributed to Mary no longer frightens us. It has a relative and subordinate sense, as a participation in the unique mediation of Christ. Certainly, given Mary's universal mission, it has an extension that it does not have in any other human creature.

In the light of this concept, not only do we not hesitate to call Mary Mediatrix of All Graces, but we also call the apostles, missionaries, those who preach or witness to the Gospel mediators. Pastors, parents who educate their children in the Christian faith, and catechists are all mediators. Whoever exercises some form or another of the apostolate, even in that precious and hidden form which is the apostolate of prayer and suffering is a mediator. It is clear in all these cases that we are dealing with a form of mediation that is subordinate to and dependent on that of Christ, who never ceases to be the unique mediator by the fact that he makes others participants in this, his prerogative.

These are the concepts which the Second Vatican Council very clearly sets forth precisely with regard to Mary, about whom one can say that, even if that Council did not proclaim the dogma of the universal mediation of Mary, it expressed all of the principles on which it is based. It says in fact: "the unique mediation of the Redeemer does not exclude but rather gives rise to a manifold cooperation which is but a sharing in this one source. The Church does not hesitate to profess this subordinate role of Mary which it constantly experiences and recommends to the heartfelt attention of the faithful, so that encouraged by this maternal help they may more closely adhere to the Mediator and Redeemer" (LG 62).

The extension of the participation of Mary in the mediation of Christ is proportionate to the participation that she had in all the works of the Redeemer and in the mission that she is still carrying out as our mother. Saints and theologians insist that we have received Christ, the fount of every grace, from Mary. Thus we also receive all the graces that come to us through her. Her divine maternity — and it is always a good thing to keep this in mind — is the principal source of all the works of Mary and hence even of her mediation.

The mission that Mary is now carrying out toward humanity is summed up in this way by the Second Vatican Council: "Taken up to heaven she did not lay aside this saving office but by her manifold intercession continues to bring us the gifts of eternal salvation." And again: "She cares for the brethren of her Son who still journey on earth, surrounded by dangers and difficulties, until they are led into their blessed home" (LG 62). These expressions are very clear and render it legitimate to call Mary Mediatrix of All Graces, when the significance of her dependence and participation in the unique mediation of Christ is well understood. For this reason the Christian people have always had recourse to Mary in every necessity.

Reflections

About Mary — It is clear that every Marian title does not obscure but throws light on the mission of salvation and grace which comes from Christ. The official texts of the Church contain with clarity the foundations for calling Mary Mediatrix of All Graces. Other than the citations from Vatican II which we have reported, we recall: *Adiutricem populi* of Pope Leo XIII (1895); *Ad diem illum* of St. Pope Pius X (1904); *Miserentissimus* of Pope Pius XI (1928); and the radio message of Pope Pius XII on May 13, 1946.

About us — We must understand both the extension and the limits of the Marian titles. We should never fear that, praising Mary, we subtract something from Jesus. Quite the opposite. We glorify the source of all the goods received from Mary. Let us invoke the Virgin with faith; the fact that she intercedes to obtain for us every grace is not a major difficulty but a major help in obtaining them.

A Mother Who Keeps the Family Together

"I am the good shepherd... and I offer my life for my sheep. I have other sheep who are not of this fold, and I must lead them, and they will listen to my voice, and there will be one flock, one shepherd" (Jn 10:11-16). This is Jesus' great dream: that there be one flock just as there is only one Lord, one faith, one baptism. Today the problem of ecumenism, of the unity of all Christians, is very much alive, even though very far from a solution. The Lord prayed that we might become one, as he and the Father are one, so that our union will be a motive for the world's coming to believe in Jesus Christ (cf. Jn 17:21). Instead, Christians present themselves as scandalously divided. How can this be?

A first division took place during the time of Nestorius. Against his teaching, the Council of Ephesus, in 431, defined the fact that in Christ there was one person with two natures, human and divine, and that Mary was the Mother of the person of Christ, God and man, and hence the Mother of God. Nestorianism exists to this day. In 1054 there was the great schism of the Eastern Orthodox Churches for reasons which we find hard to understand today. After another nearly five hundred years we arrive at the great split of the Protestant reform in 1517, followed shortly thereafter, in 1534, by the separation of the Anglicans. From that time on the splintering is beyond counting, creating ever deeper furrows weighted down by wars, persecutions and discrimination. It is now a veritable Babel. Confronting it one asks, just who are these Christians, the true followers of Jesus?

Today contacts are sought through dialogue. The encounters between the pope and the Patriarch Athenagoras, then with the Primate of the Anglican Church, and the World Council of Churches are famous. It seems that only the pope is asking pardon for all the mistakes of the past. It is a fact that he alone, with his spiritual ascendancy, thought to invite all the religions to a meeting in Assisi, and to program another for the year 2000. But without a lot of prayer and conversion on the part of all, as Vatican II points out, there will never be any unity. For this reason we see the Octave of Prayer for Unity as one of the most beautiful and fruitful initiatives which is observed each year from the 18th to the 25th of January. Still the divisions continue to smolder, even on the occasion of certain encounters. I recall, in 1984, an Anglican pilgrimage to Lourdes. There were prayers in common, but then, for the Eucharistic celebration, the Anglicans assisted politely at the Catholic Mass without taking an active part. How sad!

What role does Mary have in the ecumenical movement? Is she the mother of unity or a motive for division? Pope Leo XIII does not hesitate to affirm: "The cause of the union of Christians belongs specifically to the spiritual maternity of Mary." But is this so? Outwardly one notes a certain rigidity and positions so distant as to seem to be without solution. Then if we dig a little deeper, we see that the real differences have to do not so much with Mary, but with the idea of Church, the function of the papacy, the interpretation of Sacred Scripture which, left to individual freedom, can be transformed into an instrument of perdition as St. Peter warns us (2 P 3:16): "In them [Paul's letters] there are some things hard to understand that the ignorant and unstable distort to their own destruction, just as they do the other scriptures."

This is an actual fact: the whole Protestant world, confronted by a pontificate so markedly Marian as is that of Pope John Paul II, feels obliged to study once again the figure of Mary. For many, Luther's commentary on the *Magnificat* has been a happy discovery.

Above all, the wall of silence surrounding the figure of Mary weighs heavily. Brother Roger Schutz, the very open Calvinist founder of Taizé, clearly affirms: "After four centuries of division, the conspiracy of silence maintained around Mary renders every meeting of minds impossible. At the beginning of the Reform this conspiracy of silence did not exist." It is a silence that is gradually being overcome on the common basis of the Bible. But the way is arduous and long. It is not as when several political parties are forced to agree in order to form a government: one cedes a little here and the other a little there in order to arrive at a common program. Here it is another thing altogether and tactics don't count.

The way to union begins with the certainty that it is Christ who wants it. Conversations allow for many clarifications because, after centuries of separation, each one is loaded with prejudices about the other, attributing to them ideas which they do not have and ignoring existing realities. When, speaking to Catholics, we announce that among the Protestants there are convents of Sisters (for example, The Sisters of Mary), that there are Benedictine and Franciscan monasteries, the listeners look amazed, hearing things that they had never imagined. Even more is this the case when one speaks of Mary to Protestants, naturally on the basis of Sacred Scripture. When this is done, however, we find that it is not uncommon to see Protestant families in prayer at Marian sanctuaries.

The Protestant position with respect to Mary varies widely. From the very beginning we notice differences between Luther, Calvin and Zwingli. Let us repeat that, for the most part, there is no difficulty with respect to the first great Marian dogmas which preceded any division: Mary, mother of God and ever virgin. The most recent dogmas are either denied or left to the free interpretation of each one. But where the difference is the strongest has to do with her cult which for too many centuries Protestants have abandoned. And we must confess that, also on the part of Catholics, the cult of the Blessed Virgin is ever in need of being purified of excesses and elements which have corrupted it.

Let us conclude with these optimistic words of Pope Paul VI: "Love for the mother of the Lord must sensitize us to the apprehensions and to the goals of the ecumenical movement, above all, since the Catholic faithful are united to the faithful of the Orthodox Churches in venerating the glorious *Theotókos* (Mother of God), and in calling her the *Hope of Christians*. They are united with the Anglicans, whose classic theologians threw light on the solid scriptural basis of the cult of the Mother of the Lord, and her contemporary theologians increasingly underscore the importance of the place that Mary occupies in the Christian life. And they are united to the Churches of the Reform in which love for Sacred Scripture, in glorifying God with the very words of the Virgin, flourishes with such vigor" (*Marialis cultus*, 32). The document of Pope Paul VI ends affirming that the cult of the Virgin is the way that leads to Christ, source and center of all ecclesial communion.

Reflections

About Mary — A true knowledge of Mary leads to unity. Every mother is the source of union between the members of the same family. Unity is a gift of God which must be implored with many prayers. And for this reason it is necessary to incessantly ask for Mary's intercession.

About us — We must feel this problem at our own level, and not leave it to the responsibility of those "whose job it is." On the part of the faithful it will be useful to pray for this purpose, inform themselves about the progress made, participate more intensely if possible in the annual Octave of Prayer, look with love upon all the followers of Christ, sharing with them his sigh: that there be but one flock under one shepherd.

Finally we invite all to repeat the beautiful prayer of Brother Roger Schutz: "O God, you willed to make the Virgin Mary the figure of the Church. She received Christ and gave him to the world. Send upon us your Holy Spirit so that, very soon, we will be visibly united in one body so that we can radiate Christ to all men who cannot now believe."

This book was designed and published by St. Pauls/
Alba House, the publishing arm of the Society of St.
Paul, an international religious congregation of priests
and brothers dedicated to serving the Church through
the communications media. For information regarding
this and associated ministries of the Pauline Family of
Congregations, write to the Vocation Director, Society
of St. Paul, 7050 Pinehurst, Dearborn, Michigan 48126
or check our internet site, www.albahouse.org